This is for Alex

I have a song to sing,
and heaven will hear me

Pretty Women Curse,
Ugly Men Sing

**The Enosh Rhapsodies:
Book One**

The Divine Image

To Mercy, Pity, Peace, and Love
All pray in their distress;
And to these virtues of delight
Return their thankfulness.

For Mercy, Pity, Peace, and Love
Is God, our father dear,
And Mercy, Pity, Peace, and Love
Is Man, his child and care.

For Mercy has a human heart,
Pity a human face,
And Love, the human form divine,
And Peace, the human dress.

Then every man, of every clime,
That prays in his distress,
Prays to the human form divine,
Love, Mercy, Pity, Peace.

And all must love the human form,
Where Mercy, Love, and Pity dwell
There God is dwelling too.

by William Blake

01:01 *Lost Sheep and Salesman*

These towers dot the skyline of an impossible city in the distance. They're so massive, yet so out of reach. So uniform and ordered, yet messy and chaotic. They reach for the sky, yet sit on the water, and glow with embedded clusters of sleepless windows. Pouring bright siren's song into the night, across crashing water, yet silent from this distance. Enosh, a young boy sitting in the backseat of his grandpa's car, can only answer the call of all those distant lights with his wondrous gaze.

Enosh: I wanna be there one day.
Pa: *rouses from behind his firm grip on the steering wheel, glancing over at the window,* Oh, you don't want to live there, son. It's not a place for Christian folk.
Enosh: *furrows brows, spinning the gears beneath them to a conclusion that doesn't quite catch,* Why's that Pa?
Pa: *takes a moment to carefully pick out the phrasing of his words,* That's simple, son: Ezekiel 34.
Enosh: What does that mean?
Pa: *sighs,* Don't you read the bible?

[01:01~Lost Sheep and Salesman]

Enosh: Not that part.
Pa: Alright, son, there's only two kinds of people that survive in that city: Salesman and Lost Sheep.
Enosh: *lets his gears start grinding again,* Which am I, Pa?
Pa: Neither.
Enosh: Why's that?
Pa: 'Cause you're not gonna live there. Not while I'm alive, and on this Earth.
Enosh: Why can't I live there?
Pa: *takes a deep breath,* That place—those people, they eat eachother up like animals.
Enosh: Do the salesman eat the sheep?
Pa: No. The sheep eat each other, the salesman watch.
Enosh: But sheep oughta eat grass.
Pa: That's why they're lost, son.
Enosh: What makes them so lost?
Pa: Some have lost Jesus, so they aint got no shepherd. *takes a moment to think,* Most have false shepherds.
Enosh: *looks off to the window, eyebrows relaxed, gears catching,* The salesman?
Pa: *glances into the rear-view mirror, speaks through a proud smile,* That's right, son. Real

sharp. *nods, continuing,* They own all the money, sell all the houses, all the food, all the clothes, all the cars, just like that, they sell all the sheep too.

Enosh: What makes them so bad?

Pa: A good shepherd is like Jesus, son. Selfless, humble, generous. *wrinkles his nose,* Salesmen are fat, selfish, and greedy. They don't care about feeding the herd. It's never 'what can I do for my sheep?', with them, it's always 'what can those sheep do for me?'

Enosh: Is uncle Sammy a sheep?

Pa: *draws out a sigh,* Sam'll come home someday.

Enosh: Why can't Sam be a salesman?

Pa: *blinks rapidly into the mirror.* Don't you go getting any ideas.

Enosh: I'm not, I just wanna know.

Pa: Alright. *takes a breath to think,* Two things keep lost sheep from being salesman, Sammy's a good man, that's one.

Enosh: What's the other one?

Pa: Son, you ask too many questions.

Enosh: I promise, this'll be the last one.
Pa: *nods,* Alright. *thinks it over,* Alright, I'll tell you. But I'll need a minute.

So the minutes pass by. The car rolling down traffic in time with the floating towers passing by their windows. Enosh seeing lanterns dotting the night sky with hopes and dreams, where Pa sees the work-lights of misinformed miners, working toward gold they'll never see; Pa seeing overgrown tombstones sitting on Hell, where Enosh sees towers reaching into Heaven; Enosh seeing his future, where Pa sees his past.

Pa: Most people aren't smart enough to see, let alone use, the 'Trick of the Trader'.
Enosh: What's that?
Pa: Ah-ah, you said that was your last question. A good Christian man keeps his word.
Enosh: *crosses arms over his chest, locking them in place, gears whirring incessantly,* That's not fair.
Pa: *mumbles,* Life's not fair.
Enosh: Isn't a Pa supposed to be fair, as a 'good Christian'?
Pa: Hmm, *nods,* Alright, I'll tell ya if you're so fixed on it.

Enosh smiles, listening intently.

Pa: Half of it's about saying you'll give one thing, while sweeping the truth of that lie under the rug. The other half is about keeping it under the rug, long enough to pull it out from under someone who never saw the rug in the first place. That way, they can't get back at you.
Enosh: *furrows brows,* Huh?
Pa: In all those medicine commercials, who buys all that medicine? Old folks, and you know old folks don't have the best ears, don't you?
Enosh: That's right, they don't.
Pa: Then why do salesman always tack on all those risks and side-effects at the backend of 'em, an' read 'em in quiet voices, going three words a second?
Enosh: I dunno.
Pa: They do it so that if you get sick from their pills, they can say it was your own damn fault. *wrinkles his nose,* What matters, to them, is keeping your money.
Enosh: I'm not sure I understand.
Pa: *sighs,* You like happy meals, son?

Enosh: Should I...are they bad?
Pa: *has a small chuckle,* I'm not trying to scare you, son, I'm just telling ya the truth.
Enosh: I like them.
Pa: *nods,* You saw them on the telovee right?
Enosh: Mhmm.
Pa: Why is it that they put toys in 'em, hmm? Why is it shaped like a present, and any-time they're on the telo, all you see is kids playing and happy, instead of seeing the food the whole time?
Enosh: *thinks it over.*
Pa: I'll tell you. They do it because they want you to think about everything except what they're actually selling you—a cheap patty, with old pickle-slices and packaged ketchup, that you feed your kids so that this great nation gets raised on heart disease for the price of a three-dollar three-piece meal. *lets his face crease, voice grim,* That, son, is the Trick of the Trader.
Enosh: *nods,* I think I get it now. *takes a few moments to think over everything he's heard, before his*

gears finally catch and pick up again.

Which are you, Grandpa?
Pa: I'm a shepard, son. I'm your shepard.

01: 02 *The Barren Oak*

He's buried in front of an Oak tree, rooted in a high hill, overlooking a withering lake house. He'd held his Bible so close to his heart, in life, that his family had thought it only natural to bury him with it resting on the center of his chest. His tombstone lovingly inscribed, *My epitaph? That's easy, John 10:11.*

The Oak is thick, strong but leafless—waiting for the right day of Spring to live again, in a different layer of rugged timber skin. Strong but leafless—he waits. Watching the lakehouse. Waiting for sleepless windows to dim.

Twilight pours over the hillside, breaking against his tombstone, it blankets a shadow over the Oak's side. Therein, the supernatural shepherd rests his shoulder against its shaded trunk. Flipping through the Bible he carried with him into the after-life, one last time. He stops on the last page. Therein, he's placed pictures over the years. Some of his wife, some of his two sons and daughter Clara. The one he holds out, picking it from the rest, is one of him and his son, Sammy. A photo of him, as he'd like to hold him in memory—still young; still home.

He flips his Bible shut, looking to his withered home, one last time. His eyelids sinking with the setting of a sun in the distance. A red car roars like a vicious beast in the distance, searing his eyelids open as it tears down-road toward his home. It burns the twilight into a summer scene, bursting from the photo held in the Shepherd's hand. In this twilight, it blossoms from the treads of this car, roaring afront the Shepherd's aged and shaded eyes.

    The smell of tantalizing franks and burgers waft into the room, under the pang of Ma's lit cigar. A mingling taste of burning meat, smoke, and a far off placid lake permeates the air between Sammy, a young man with shame draped over a gaunt face, and the shadow of his Mother, a strong woman with piercing eyes, at a younger age than the Shepherd has seen in some time.

    A Box of Jewelry sits between them.

    Sammy: *in a hushed voice,* I meant to tell you sooner.
    Ma: *exhales smoke almost deliberately in Sam's direction,* Before or after?
    Sammy: *keeping his voice,* Please. Just don't tell Pa.
    Ma: *nods mad-as-hell,* Oh I'm telling him, soon as all the folks leave. No point in souring his good mood while it lasts. *points her cigar at Sammy's chest.* What's your plan, huh? Take your Ma's jewelry box and make a break for it?

Sammy: *stares at the wooden floor, jaw clenched,*
Ma: Do I need to get your Father in here?
Sammy: *sighs in defeat,* We needed it, to make it to the city.
Ma: *nods, a little less mad-as-hell,* So you expect to just have it your way in the city, huh? Raise it there too I imagine?
Sammy: I'm not ready, Ma.
Ma: *grimaces,* What's that mean? What—You not man enough?
Sammy: I'm not old enough, *fear of the future gathers in tears at the corners of his eyes,* I'm only nineteen.
Ma: You were damn old enough to get the deed done, weren't you? Felt like a real man, biting forbidden fruit, stealing out your own mama's purse, but when it comes time to own up to what being a man *really* gets you—
Sammy: *breaks down, sobbing between his palms,* What do you expect me to do?!
Ma: What do I expect? What do *I* expect?! *leans over, smacking the hands from Sammy's face.* I expect you to be a fuckin' man and own

up to the fact that you went and got this girl pregnant!
Sammy: Please! Please, just keep it quiet. I know I messed up. Please, just not here.
Ma: *breathes deeply, settling back into her seat while dashing her cigar. sighs,* Alright...alright. Just think, alright, what's the plan?
Sammy: The plan?
Ma: You're having a baby. Where you gonna raise it? How you gonna raise it? The city's expensive. *slides the box across the table, dashing out her cigar completely.* This box won't get you past a month.
Sammy: *grips the box at its edges with white-knuckles...*we won't need a month.
Ma: *furrows brows.*
Sammy: We wasn't goin' to the city to raise no child Ma.
Ma: *seeing her son through slitted eyes,* Be careful what you let out your mouth.
Sammy: We was...takin' care of the problem.

Ma almost smacks the shame off Sammy's face,

but Pa walks in just at that moment, too drunk and cheery to see tension.

Pa: Sammyboy! Come on out, I want a picture with ya out on the water.
Sammy: *shifts eyes between Pa's grin and Ma's grimace,* Sure, as long as it's okay with Ma.
Ma: *stands with cold eyes settling over her son, the sweat on his back chilling his spine.* I wouldn't want to sour Pa's good mood.

Pa and Sammy exit out to the back porch.

Ma: *picks her cigar up, moving to light it again.*
She ignites once, her hand shaking slightly. Twice, it doesn't catch. Another, and another, and another, until the scene fades.

The night darkens with the final gasps of Heaven's light sinking under Earth in a dying twilight. The Shepherd takes a single step toward his old home, before a set of spindly fingers dig into his shoulder, stabbing through his decaying sinews.

He breaks into a run, sinking with every step. Another set of dagger-like fingertips dig into his shins and thighs, then knees and mid-section. His sinking progression in time with the slow death of the

day in the distance. He goes on, reaching for that damned car, pulling up to his front porch. A hand clasps itself over his face and the land of the living sinks away. Gone.
    The dead Oak watches on in silence.
    The day has ended, and night's reign begins.

01:03 *Gutted in the Open Air*

  Behind the sleepless windows of that lake house rests a dining room. At its center, hidden under a blue cloth and transparent plastic covering, is a table carved from a once great sequoia tree. In a past life having held up the stars with its foliage. Now holding up a half dozen steaming pots of assorted dinner foods for the savages that had wrestled him onto his knees. He's stripped of his foliage coat and proud posture, shaped into a kneeling piece of woodwork from a towering goliath. But a fine piece of furniture he was, under that cloth and plastic covering. His sculpted face hidden from view.
  All of the doors have been shut, to keep out the cold night air. The water running under the back porch is placid, awaiting a breeze to ripple waves over its cheek. On the inside, the scent of roasted chicken, mashed potatoes, cream-like gravy, boiled eggs, and homestyle fries are warming the room where four people surround the sequoia.
  Among them is Ma, the lines of her face showing at least ten years of added age, the puffiness of recent sobs adding on some more. As well as Aunt Lilith and Uncle Abraham, who are paired in description, as they are rarely seen separate in public. The former being a petite woman with full lips and intelligent eyes, who hangs on her husband's arm whenever able. The latter of which being a large man with large hands, and broad features. The head of the table is left empty. The three of them are seated across from each

other. Lilith and Abraham together, Ma seated lonesome.

Then there is Enosh, who sits by his window off to the side. It looks over the idlying water of the lake and those far off stars that float on a larger lake in the distance. He reads the Bible his grandfather had given him, in his favorite spot, on the night of his passing.

Ma: *settles into her seat with a damp napkin held in hand,* I'm not in an eating mood, but I made so much. Eat. Please.
Lilith: *nods for Abe to get the first plate,*
Abe: Shouldn't Enosh come over to eat?
Ma: *waves the thought away,* He's always reading. See him there, *gestures over to Enosh scribbling something into his bible,* he's making all of those notes cause he's got a real active mind. Almost a man now, fourteen.
Lilith: That's a handsome thing for a young man to have, he might just fill in a few gaps in this old house.
Ma: *sighs,* He just might.
Abe: *stares down at his food as he eats,*
Lilith: *places a hand on Ma's,* I'm sure it can't be easy to be without

a man in the house, if you need anything, we're here.
Ma: *nods, patting the top of Lilith's hand,* I've lost so many people, *sighs,* everything and everyone gets ripped from my fingertips. At one point, or another.
Abe: *looks into his mother's pained eyes, shifting his shoulders from broad to slopped, a hand coming to her shoulder,* If you gotta cry, cry on me Ma. I've got too much I coulda done, but did none, and I—*we're* gonna take care of ya the best we can.
Lilith: *nods in understanding.*
Ma: *pats Abe's hand, grins lightly,* You were always his favorite. That reminds me. *snaps her fingers,* Enosh.
Enosh: *looks up from his bible, placing his pencil down in the spine.*
Ma: I wanna see that little note Pa put in there for ya, over his favorite script.
Enosh: *nods,* John 10:11?
Ma: *grins,* That's the one.
Enosh: *flips a few pages in his book, recites calmly,* I am the good shepherd—

Ma: *snaps fingers, grin faltering,* I know the scripture, boy. I want to see what he wrote.
Enosh: *looks back down, recites less calmly,* Son, I am your shepherd and—
Ma: *snaps fingers, frustrated, face straight,* I know what he wrote, I want to *see* it.
Enosh: *stands,* Could I just get something from my room first?
Ma: *seeing her grandson through slitted eyes.* Come here.
Enosh: But Ma—
Ma: I don't want no buts, except *your* butt right here.
Enosh: *eyes pleading,* Ma...
Ma: Now, Enosh.

He walks over with a sigh, closing his bible over a pencil in the spine, he hands it to Ma. She flips it open, her eyes passing over it for a moment before going wide with disbelief.

Enosh: *sees Ma's face contort into a grimace, tearing up,*
Abe: *moves to chime in, stopped by the tug of his wife's hand on the back of his shirt,*
Lilith: *shakes head, speaks without moving her lips,*

For a few moments, the room is silent as a monastery—only the distant sound of a muscle car tearing down a far off road is heard alongside a grumbling storm in the distance and the sounds of owls and crickets in the night, outside of this moment. It feels isolated, at peace, before the silence is cracked open by the wet sound of flesh smacking against flesh, followed by the pound of something hard being smacked down onto the table, shaking the sequoia's veins.

Enosh lies on the floor, silently sobbing with a hand over half of his face, rubbing the tingling pain from his reddened cheek.

Ma settles back into her seat with a deep breath, her plate broken by the force of Enosh's bible being slammed down on it—all spread out in front of her. Though it's clear to see this wasn't any "Bible" at all. The leather cover being it's only guise as it looks to have been crudely skinned from the Bible Pa had handed down to Enosh. This book was no holy book in this house, in fact it was as far from that as it could be. It was a book on the stock market titled, *The Intelligent Investor*, stuffed into the Bible's skin like a thanksgiving turkey.

    Ma: Thank God your Pa never saw you done such a thing. Damn well would of ripped his heart from him as bad as it was. *shakes her head in slow mounting disappointment,* Is there more?
    Enosh: *says nothing.*

Ma: I promise you, you'll get a good lick for every single one I find. Best tell me now.
Enosh: *sniffles*...Yes.
The sound of the muscle car draws nearer.
Lightning strikes.
Ma: Where?
Enosh:...the bed...inside the mattress.
Ma: *sighs*, Alright, alright. Here's what we're gonna do: You're gonna go upstairs. In the morning you'll give me all of 'em, and I'm burning them—Every. Single. One. And you better have a hold of your Pa's bible, *raises a hand shaking with passion,* or I swear-to-the-lord.

Enosh stands up, nods, then makes his way up the stairs.

Ma: *sighs deeply.* I'm sorry, I shouldn't of done that here. Not tonight.
Lilith: You don't need to apologize.
Abe: That's how we was raised, after all.
Ma: *nods thoughtfully,* That's what worries me.

Lilith: Howso?
Ma: The boy takes after his father—

The door swings open, a man stands in the doorway, his red muscle car in the background. All the eyes in the room fall on him. The man is tall and gaunt, with chiseled features, silver aviator sunglasses shielding his eyes. A red leather jacket hangs around his shoulders. He holds a lit cigarette in his hand and puffs it as he stalks into the room, usurping the seat at the head of the table.

Abe: *grimaces,* That's not your place. You got no right to that.
Red: You gon' take it then, junior? *smirks,* I'd like to see you try.
Abe: *clenches a fist under the table.*
Red: *puffs his cigarette, shakes head slowly, leaning back into his chair,* I was hoping you'd grown some balls since getting married. Best not get a divorce, you might just go from an outie to an innie.

Abe almost bolts out of his seat, only stopped by his wife's calm fingers lacing into his clenched fist, and her hand's firm hold of his shoulder.
Again, Lilith speaks without moving her lips.

Ma: When'd you start smoking?
Red: Sometime after you.
Ma: *raises an eyebrow,* Gettin' smart with me now?
Red: Nah, nah, just honest. *blows smoke in Ma's direction,* aren't you always honest?
Lilith: *forces a smile,* So you're Sammy, then?
Sam: It's just Sam. I'm—
Ma: Broke and need money.
Sam: No.
Ma: *breathes deeply,* Hell, you must be lost, then.
Sam: *looks Ma square in the eyes,* You know damn well why I'm here.
Ma: If you came to pay your father some respects, you missed that boat a long time ago. Lake's out back, you can get swimming if it'll help you sleep at night.
Sam: *nods, pursing lips, sucks teeth,* I'm here to get what's mine.
Ma: What do you want that I haven't given you? What in the world could I have left for you to take?
Sam: *puts cigarette out on the plastic covering,* My goddamn son.

01:04 *The Storm Breaks*

The room is dimly lit and spacious. With a mattress at its heart that has been cut open along the side. Sheets made up of grey pelt blankets and thick white wool are spread over the floor. They're loosely blanketed over cover-less books that range from adult fiction, to scientific journals, to biographies, to books about wall street, to mysteries, tragedies and the like. A common thread among all of them being uniform dashes, circles, and side-notes written in Enosh's neat handwriting.

He sits by a window overlooking the sleepless stars in the distance. They glow just beyond his reach, some hundreds of miles away. If he'd had a boat he'd sail straight to it. Right across that small placid lake into the churning Hudson. Hell, if there wasn't a raging storm outside these walls, he would walk the distance. Because he knew more than anything else, he wanted that dream in his hand, at this moment—rather than hundreds of miles past his fingertips.

With a little help, he tells himself, *with the right chance*, he prays, *I could get there.*

**Lightning strikes,
sparking the outline of sycamore tree branches in his window,
swinging into view, they beat against the lakehouse side.**

Enosh: I know what I've got to do.
takes a moment before acting with automatic confidence, grabs a bag out from his closet, begins filling it with clothes and books, the last of which being the skinned Bible his grandfather had handed to him.

Ma: You're not taking him with you.
Sam: *sees his mother through slitted eyes,* Is that so?
Lilith: *nods to her husband,*
Abe: *places a hand on his brother's shoulder,* This ain't your house, son. Best leave now.
Sam: *shrugs the hand from his shoulder, leaning toward his brother,* Who's gon' make me, junior?
flicks his cigarette into Abe's chest.

The two men stand from the table

Abe: *towers over Sam.*
Sam: *smiles,* You think you're all big and tough. Just think you can talk like the old man and I'll piss myself, huh? *takes out a lighter and another cigarette,* Don't make me

embarrass you in front of your wife.
Abe: *grimaces,* Don't test me.
Sam: Relax junior, just think of what jesus would do. *lights cigarette,* Then sit the fuck down.
Abe: *smacks the cigarette from Sam's lips, knocking his aviators to the table.*
Lilith: *grabs her husband at the sleeve,*
Abe: *jerks his arm loose of his wife's hold, pressing a finger into Sam's chest,* You best leave, now. Before I stop being polite.
Sam: *sucks teeth,* Cut the shit. Sit down, before I get serious.
Lilith: Sweetheart. Sit down and let them deal with it.
Ma: Why did he have to come home?
Lilith: Don't let him get the best of you.
Ma: We should all just sit down. Alright? Both of you.
Abe: *grimaces,* What if I don't wanna sit down. *takes a step away from his wife, up to Sam.*
Lilith: Abraham. Sit down.

Sam: *takes out another cigarette,* Best listen to your master there, Junior.
Abe: *stares Sam down,* You're stoned.
Sam: You're whipped.
Abe: Don't make me hurt you.
Ma: Both of you are in my house—
Sam: Oh yea? You sure you wanna do this?
Abe: Yea, *grabs his brother by the collar of his shirt,* I do.
Lilith: Abraham...
Sam: Come on, then. I ain't got all night to hear you bark.
Lilith: *stands, placing a hand on her husband's shoulder.*
Abe: *clenches fist,* I'll show you a bark.
Lilith: *leans over. whispers something in Abe's ear.*
Abe: *shrinks back, releasing the collar.*
Sam: *grins, mocking,* cuh-tshh.
Abe: I think we should go home. *looks to his wife.*
Lilith: *nods,* We'll leave. *looks to Ma,* I'm so sorry, we don't want to escalate the situation anymore than it has to.

Ma: Lilith, there's no need for that, if anything—
Lilith: No really, *hands her husband his jacket*, it's getting late. Thanks for dinner, though.

despite Ma's instistance, the couple awkwardly make their way out of the front door.

Ma: *sighs*, you need to leave.
Sam: I'm gone as soon as Enosh's in my passenger seat.
Ma: *raises an eyebrow*, Do you want to make me call the police on my own son, the day his father got put in the ground? *takes a shaken voice*, Are you really that cold? You want that much attention? Cause if that's it, come back tomorrow. I'd hope to have raised you into enough of a man not kick your own mother while she's down.
Sam: *nods thoughtfully*, Alright. You've got a few points there.
Ma: Got a smoke?
Sam: I thought you quit.
Ma: I quit for Abraham. That man gave all his years, I wanted to give him more of mine. *gestures*

over the interior of the withering lakehouse, Look what that got me.
Sam: *hands Ma a cigarette and lighter,*
Ma: *lights up, puffs smoke.*
Sam: *waits a moment before awkwardly leaning over to plant a kiss on Ma's temple, whispers,*...I love you.
Ma: *sighs smoke,* I love you too, Samuel. *nods to the door,* now get the fuck out of my house.

The storm breaks outside, from a raging torrent to a calm drizzle.

01:05 *Acting up and Ugly Cracks*

The night is black as charcoal dust—It wraps itself around the shoulders of waving trees as a thick blanket of cold, rather than against it. Hiding small droplets, that tap themselves over puddles forgotten by a raging flood of falling water. The blanket is dotted with clusters of stars and constellations. The lake is placid and the road is empty, except for a red muscle car.

Hidden away under a branch, is a young Woodcock. It chirps a melody that blends with the shifting life of night, as it hops and skips toward a nest. From a far off patch of shade, slips a black-feathered Nighthawk. It weaves itself past branch after branch, advancing steadily. The small bird stumbles into the nest.

Down below, Sam walks out of the withering lakehouse and over to his car. He slips his silver aviators back on, before easing into the driver's seat. It doesn't take him more than an instant to realize the rain-soaked boy huddled up in his passenger's seat.

Sam: *shuts the door,* Well, I'll be damned.
Enosh: I can explain—
Sam: *turns over the ignition,*
Enosh: *raises an eyebrow, gears not quite catching,* You're not sending me back?
Sam: Nope. *pulls off the front porch,*

Enosh: *feels a twist, a pinch in his stomach, he grabs the steering wheel,* Wait!

Sam: *stops car, glancing over a set of soaked clothes, and a stuffed backpack currently ruining his leather passenger seat,* You're running away, aren't you?—I know a runaway pack when I see one.

Enosh: *nods slowly, pulling his hands away...*yea.

Sam: *thinks a moment,* First time?

Enosh: *nods.*

Sam: If you're having second thoughts, the door's right there.

Enosh: *grabs the passenger door handle,*

Sam: *safety locks the doors,* You've just gotta tell me somethin' first.

Enosh: *nods,* Okay, I can do that.

Sam: *brushes a hand over Enosh's cheek, the flesh purpling over blue,* How often does she hurt you like this?

Enosh: *shrinks away,* Not too often. Just when I act up, that's all.

Sam: *sucks teeth,* What's actin' up in there, nowadays?

Enosh: ...

Sam: *nods,* Alright. Tell you what—I'll show you mine, and you tell me yours.
Enosh: *raises an eyebrow,*
Sam: *takes off jacket, pulling down his shirt collar, to show a grey scar stretching over his shoulder and down to just over where his heart should be.*
Enosh: *blinks rapidly,*
Sam: *nods with a wry grin,* I tell dames it was an accident sailing down in the caribbean. Truth is, I can't even swim.
Enosh: *looks up into his uncle's eyes, gears whirring,* How'd it *really* get there?
Sam: *grin falters, letting the shirt collar come back up to his neck,* Just be glad you never saw your Ma drink hard liquor.
Enosh: *wipes the rainwater from his brow,* What'd you do?
Sam: *sighs,* When I was about your age, I took a girl into the priest's box and did some...unholy things. *chuckles short,* her father almost killed me. When I got home, Ma tried to beat 'em to it—came at me with a bottle, it

broke, I got a mean cut. *shrugs*, It happens.
Enosh: *stares at the droplets speckling the windshield,* I'm so sorry.
Sam: hmm, what're you apologizing for? *pokes the boy in the arm,* Doubt you could even hold a jameson with those toothpicks.
Enosh: No, really...that's awful.
Sam: *waves the idea away like second-hand smoke,* I just got a bum deal. First son, she got better after she saw what a failure that kind of meanness turns out.
Enosh: *furrows brows,* You're not a failure, Uncle Sammy. You drive nice cars, you date pretty women, you do whatever you want, whenever you want, and no one can tell you what's what. *sighs,* What I wouldn't give for that.
Sam: *smiles, ruffling up the boy's wet hair,* You're your father's son.
Enosh: *shrinks away,* You knew my father?
Sam: *stammers,* Uh-yea, we were good pals, drinking buddies, really. Real free spirit he was. *puts*

his thoughts to a stop for a second, gears turning in reverse.
Enosh: Was he drunk...when it happened?
Sam: When what happened?
Enosh: The car crash, when I was a baby, and they...
Sam: *smiles, gears catching, before realizing the tone of the situation and instantly wiping that smile from his face,* Right, yea. He had his issues, son. Shame your Ma had to go that way. Clara was, *sighs, staring off,* real bright.
Enosh:...Did she like to read?
Sam: Oooh yea, she loved the books. Studied the bible like no one else, even Pa was impressed every once in a while.
Enosh: What about...other books.
Sam: *scratches face,* Yea, once she got out of the house, yea. She loved them. *lets his face sink a bit,* She was, real smart, *sighs,* that one.
Enosh: *nods, pleased,*
Sam: *gestures to a book peeking out from his soaked pack,* I take it you like to read, then?
Enosh: *purses lips,* Yea. Ma doesn't like it, though—that's

why I've to get out of here, and get to the city.
Sam: *nods,* Think you'll have it better there, huh?
Enosh: *shrugs,* I think so.
Sam: *glances over the boy's bruised face,* She hurt you that bad over some books?
Enosh: *lets shade cover his shamed face, grabbing a book from the pack, handing it to Sam.*
Sam: *inspects the bible-wrapped book, sucks teeth, hands it back,* That'll do it.
Enosh: *puts it away,* She said she'll burn the rest. My books are the only things that give me something to look forward to, as long as I have them, I've got a chance to live in the city. Like you.
Sam: *nods thoughtfully, sucks teeth,* The truth is, nobody has a good life— no one lives. We survive, and if we can manage, we do our best to be happy while we do it. My working theory is that if you look at anyone, even the happiest of folks, look deep into their life—you'll be bound to see some ugly cracks. If you look at them long enough.
Enosh: *nods, listening intently,*
Sam: *rolls down his window, pulling out a cigarette, lights up,* You're mother told me that once, she was real

sharp, like you. *breathes smoke,* said Van Gogh only sold one painting in his life, Roosevelt was paralyzed, and Reagan had a drinking problem left over from his father. Every great man of history, from MLK to Gandhi, had a wife that got cheated on a ridiculous number of times—So, no matter who you are, there's bound to be some ugly cracks under the surface, somewhere.

 Everyone gets a bum deal. Everyone's out for themselves. It's how you deal with it that matters. Got it?

Enosh: *nods,* Got it.

 Sam: *unlocks passenger door,* So what's it gonna be?

End of Part One:
Storms on Placid Lakes

Cursing Night Begins

The Curse of Heraclitus

I am in the river,
and out of it,
I am the same,
and the opposite,

I am a mountain in the distance,
and a pebble underfoot,

I am the same,
and the opposite,
I am the world—
and I am none of it.

02:01 *Photos of Prophetic Infidelity*

    White knuckles over an old beaten up Bible. Hot air and moans leaking through the plaster of thin walls. A plastic wrapped dinner sitting on a coffee table. Photos draped over walls, that paint portraits of a broad-chested man with a chiseled jawline: In a military man's uniform, graduating, fishing with his father, at a shooting range, getting married to a petite woman with blond hair and striking blue eyes.
    They shake on the walls, in time with the peaking cries of pleasure from the room at their backs. The broad man, some years older than he looks in the hanging pictures, sits confined to a couch, flipping through his Bible. He stares intensely at the pages,

keeping his eyes off the thoughts he'd pushed deep under them. He recites verse after verse, while the seconds crawl into minutes and the moans continue, with their shaking intensity.

Some time later, there's a descent, followed by a lull. The door opens. A pierced and tattooed shadow in the doorway slips a jacket on, says some sweet nothings to the woman he leaves behind, and exits after taking a kiss on her cheek and a firm grope of her exposed rear.

The front door closes. The moaning door remains, gaping—It rings like gunshot-fire in the holy man's ears. He doesn't so much as stutter in his recitation of the verses, before he's stopped by a balmy hand brushing over his neck. A quivering kiss planted on his temple with the soft feel of shallow breath against his skin.

>**Lilith:** *whispers,* I missed you, sweetheart.
>**Abe:** *closes Bible,* Is he gone?
>**Lilith:** *smiles, nuzzling his neck,* You've got eyes, don't you?
>**Abe:** Yea, that's what I got, *shrugs her off, standing,* a good set of eyes.
>**Lilith:** *brushes her hands up to hold the sides of her husband's grim face,* What're you so upset about?
>**Abe:** You're supposed to let me know...you're supposed to tell me

when you bring your— your "guests".
Lilith: This was last minute. Besides, I knew you'd want to watch, and that freaks 'em out—big as you are.
Abe: *pulls away, pacing across the room,* Yea, real big man. That's me down to a number. *begins pointing out the pictures on the wall,* There's the big man at boot camp, real strong, a *real* nice gun there, huh?—There he is with his Pa, now that, that was a *real* man—Oh, look at this. *grabs a picture off the wall,* It's the big man in a suit—oh wait, isn't this before his tour?—that's right. *tears up...* He's getting married.
Lilith: *places a hand on her husband's shoulder,* Sweetheart, it's okay.
Abe: *puts both hands over the photo frame,* It's not. *hands tensing up, eyes brimming on sobs with every passing moment,* I'*m* not. *stares down at the picture,* I could've lost anything, Lily. Anything; My hands, my feet, my legs, my face—I'd trade it all, *shakes, crushing the photo in his large hands,* just to have my *fucking* manhood.
Lilith: At least you came home.

Abe: What home have I got where a man can walk right in and sleep with my wife?
Lilith: *brings his eyes to hers,* It's just sex. I love you, and only you. *tip-toes up to plant a kiss on his lips,* All those men in the Bible, from Jacob to David, they all had sex with other women. That didn't mean they loved their wives any less.
Abe: What am I then? Leah? Some mistake you'll carry for seven years, and the rest of your life?
Lilith: No, *takes her husband by the hands,* you're Sarah. You're my Sarah.
Abe: *pulls away,* You need to stop.
Lilith: Stop what?
Abe: I'm your husband.
Lilith: *looks through him, eyes chilling over,* You want me to stop having sex—Is that what you're saying right now?
Abe: For the love of God, yes.
Lilith: I can't do that.

A few tense moments pass between them.

Abe: What?
Lilith: *shrugs,* I can't. Not unless you...function.

Abe: *looks his wife over with slitted eyes.* Is that really it?
Lilith: I've always been honest with you, my dear. If you can get it done, then I'll need concubines to fill the space, and do what you can't.
Abe: *looks between his hands, looking for strength that isn't there, in those crumpled up memories,* I can't.
Lilith: You know the way it has to be then—I have a right to be happy, as a wife ought to be cared for.
Abe: *grimaces,* What if I say I'll leave?
Lilith: You're not leaving me.
Abe: How're you so sure?
Lilith: If we get a divorce, you'll have to explain why. I can't imagine you, in front of your mother, explaining this, *sweetheart.*
Abe: *shrinks back....*Alright.
Lilith: *sighs,* Why do you have to do this? *holds the side of her husband's face,* you say these crazy things, and you make me get all mean, for what?

Abe: *relaxes into her hand,* I'm sorry.
Lilith: I know this isn't easy for you, but don't you think a husband ought to keep his wife happy? For better or for worse?
Abe: *nods houndishly,* Yea, they ought to.
Lilith: Then you've been a fine husband. *kisses him lightly on the lips.*
Abe: *bows head,*
Lilith: Now, *smiles,* let's get to bed.

By the hand, Abraham is led through the bedroom door. His eyes glazed over, the sounds of moans and gunshots ringing through his ears.

He doesn't sleep.

02:02 *Moving Memories in Stagnant Pictures*

A cold door closes off this clinical room, made up of white tiles and porcelain. The shower runs at full, blasting water to cancel out whatever sounds could be heard from within. There are monochromatic photographs swirling around, painting white slates with scenes too painful to hold in memory. The largest of which is a blazing mural over the whole ceiling, a portrait of flocking seagulls that swim across a flaming orange sky.

Abraham stands in the mounted mirror at the center of all these nightmares. His chiseled face reddened tomato ripe, under droplets of sweat—his white molars embedded deep into a grey towel's hide—upper body bare—hands clasped around the sink's curved porcelain edges—ears ringing like an explosion just went off in the next room, rosy red at the tips and warm with stress.

These monochromatic nightmares sink down these walls, swirling a ravenous whirlpool up from his feet—creeping up his legs, they pierce into his body through his inner thighs, drowning his crotch—climbing through his veins. He's confined to a rising bath of boiling oil—aching inch by aching inch, it creeps up to his heart. The room begins to shrink with every beat.

He can only focus on the space between his teeth, pushing as much pressure as he can into that gray towel gritted therein—the burning orange ceiling scene sinking down, until it breaks on the top of Abe's head.

He's brought into the open air by a flaming rapture. He sits on an old back porch. The sound flooding back into his ears with the feel of a fishing pole in his hands, the tips of his toes skimming the lake's cool cheek, and Pa's soft smile. Hot oil washes from his veins in pins and needles.

> **Little Abe:** *breathes out, smiling at the flock of gulls passing over a warm sky.*
> **Pa:** That's a picture perfect sight, if ever I saw it.
> **Little Abe:** *nods,* Yea. *taking it in,* They fly like they haven't got a care in the world.
> **Pa:** 'Cept sticking together.
> **Little Abe:** Wonder what would happen if they didn't?
> **Pa:** I imagine whatever one decides he ought to break from that V, would plummet right out of the sky.
> **Little Abe:** *raises an eyebrow,* Why's that?
> **Pa:** The way I see it, we could fly too—If we weren't weighted down by it all, we'd need to fly *just* like they do, though: Together.

Little Abe: *shrugs,* We don't have wings—those'd be a grand help, too.
Pa: Bah, that doesn't make a man fly.
Little Abe: What ought to make a man fly, then? *points up to the burning sky,* Like one of those gulls.
Pa: *scratches the side of his face,* Those birds know what's what—they don't have bills to worry about, money to carry around, any taxes on their tails, or clothes over their feathers. Son—they've got nothing but each other, and that's all they need. *points up to the squawking gulls,* makes 'em so free they can fly.

The moment passes in peace for the next couple of minutes,
both of them watching twilight pass by,
before there's a knock at the screen door behind them.
It's Little Abraham's mother.

Ma: It's Sammy. They've got him locked up again.
Pa: *sighs,* What's he gotten into, now?

Ma: Hell if I know, he'll only talk to you. He's waiting on the phone, I think he wants you to make bail—Cause I'm sure as Hell not. *shuts screen door.*
Pa: *rests his pole against railing,* We'll pick this up some other day, son.

Pa exits out of the screen door. Abe is left lonesome with two fishing poles, and a fading twilight in the distance. The gulls fly off and out of sight.

Little Abe: *mumbles,* If Sam ain't around then, that is. *rests his pole on the railing, taking in the placid lake.*

The rod left behind by his father begins to shake, a breeze coming in on night air. The rustling trees seeming to whisper on shaking leaves, a cryptic mermer on Abraham's ear. Calling him to take up his father's pole.

Little Abe: *thinks a moment,* I shouldn't, *failing to tear his eyes from the rod...*I can't hold on like Pa can, strong as he is.

The pole bends—the line shooting out into the lake with the reel wheeling around with tumbles of nylon wire, out over the bent rod's neck. On and on and on, until it comes to the end of the wire's spool—the whole fishing pole jerking over the side of the railing. Caught like the flex of a whip by Little Abe's clutch.

He's jerked over the side of the railing, body flipping in mid-air and smacking into cold, hard stillwater. It soaks through his clothes, permeating the pores of his skin, and weighing him down, in a sinking panic.

A torrent swirls around him, dragging him into a whirlpool, that swirls down to the rocky floor of a dark abyss. Like a pit of jagged-glass quicksand, he's torn from this world into the next, inch by excruciating inch. Pulled further and further, with every passing breath he fails to take—and in the violence of it all, his father's rod slips from his fingers, lost in the whirlpool. Not a moment after, he's birthed into a dark room. With a single door afront his eyes.

02:03 *The Abyss of Wailing Desire*

    This world pulses at the edges, like the eyelids of a man days past a godly hour. The lighting is dim. The memory hazed.

    He's dressed in his old officer uniform, made up all grey by the haze of his nightmare. A man of war, with arms forceful as cannon-fire, shoulders broad as battering rams, legs tough as tank treads, wound just as tight. He wears a full grin on confident lips, rasping thick knuckles on a black door, standing tall and proud. This, the model of the man that Abe once was.

    It's made all the more jarring, as Abe stands off to the side—shrouded in the shadows—Too ashamed to come out, and risk letting his better self see the nightmarish figure he becomes—A broken man with arms like maggoted logs, all bent out of shape. With sloping shoulders like rotted missile silos. Legs weak as withering support beams—Shrinking into the shadows, ashamed. This, the model of what Abraham has become: a decomposed man, shaded by his own shame, but otherwise naked.

    He watches his younger self knock on the door with solid knuckles. The lucid image of flowers, shrouded in the haze of time, rising up from his better self's other hand. He rests the roses on the center of his chest. The door opens to the beaming face of a younger Lilith. As beautiful as ever. She hops right into the military man's arms, planting the warmest kiss on his lips.

Abraham watches on. Close to feeling the warmth of the embrace, like a naked homeless man in the cold, standing near a bonfire—He almost reaches out to touch her, as she was before—but he had stood in this scene enough times to know that the light of it burns his skin, and that once their eyes turn on him, this world starts to break. What follows is usually a bath of boiling hot oil down the length of his back—So he watches on, shrouded in darkness.

Lilith: *pulls away, giggling,* You're home!
Abraham: *raises an eyebrow,* Was there any doubt?
Lilith: *snakes a hand up across his chest,* None at all. I never stopped reading all your letters.
Abraham: You missed me that much?
Lilith: *slightly bites her bottom lip, fingers wrapping around the tie of his uniform,* You could say that.
Abraham: *leans down to peck a kiss on her lips, before letting himself be led into the apartment by the end of his tie.*

Abe follows the both of them, slipping through the door, passing from shadow to shadow.
They finally reach the bedroom, leaving a trail of discarded clothes and rose petals in their wake.

a bare thorny stem on the nightstand, and the two of them, naked over heavy sheets.

The pulsing intensifies with every step Abe takes

Lips pressed, hands and shallow breath gliding over exposed skin—the couple spends a few minutes taking in each other, before they're closest to moving into definitive sex.

Lilith: *pulls away by a half-arm's length,* Wait.
Abraham: Is there a problem?
Lilith: Not at all. *plants a short kiss on his lips,* I just want this to be perfect.
Abraham: *smiles,* It already is.
Lilith: I know it is, but I think it'd be even better if I have a quick shower. *begins standing up from the bed,*
Abraham: *laces a hand in hers,* I'm sure it'll be worth the wait regardless.
Lilith: *brings his hand up, kissing the top of it,* I know it will, but I don't want to feel like a smelly Ape the first time I have my husband in bed after some two years. *gently eases his hand to the*

bed sheets, It won't take more than a moment.

Lilith exits into the bathroom. The sound of the shower running at full blast rings through the door.

The faint sound of a window opening is heard from within the bathroom

Abe: *whispering old thoughts,* She must've gotten hot in there.
Abraham: *sniffs something fowl,*
Abe: *continues,* Guess she really did need that shower if these sheets smell this bad. It's like pure sweat is soaked into the threads.
Abraham: *sighs, smiling, eyes passing over the room.*
Abe: It's good to be home...
Abraham: *furrows brows, feeling a small lump under his side. he moves over to inspect the spot he'd laid in and finds a lighter.*
Abe: Lilith doesn't smoke.
Abraham: *inspects the lighter, seeing a snake wrapped around a rose, illustrated on its side. eyes go wide in disbelief, muscles tensing up, jaw clenching.*

for a few moments, he's frozen in shock.

**The pulsing at the edges of the scene intensifies,
white space takes up part of the frame**

Abe: He wouldn't—Not here...She wouldn't.

The faint sound of a window closing is heard from within the bathroom

Abe: *whispers,* Get up! Get up, you bastard! Leave, talk to her, chase him! *tears up,* For fuck's sake, *do* something!

His younger self stays there like this for a few minutes, just as helpless as the model of what he would become, watching from the shadows. The sound of the shower fades. He slips the lighter under his pillow just before Lilith walks through the bathroom door. She beams at his mortified face.
Lilith: Is something wrong?
Abe: I don't think I can do this.
Lilith: What do you mean.
Abe: *takes sheets up over himself,* I don't think I can do this, not tonight.
Lilith: *slides into bed, nuzzling up to him,* Are you okay?

Abe: *grips the lighter under his pillow, with white knuckles,* Yea, I'm just—

Abraham charges out of the shadows, bathed in boiling hot oil from head to toe. He heaves himself up to the bedside—digs his hand under his old pillow, and pulls from it the damned lighter—A red snake and rose blazing in its side—He speaks...but no words leave his moving lips...the lighter is not held in his hand, having slipped through his intangible fingers, and the intense burning of the light feels like it's searing the skin over his shoulders—he's burning up—catching fire—roasting alive.

With every beat of his racing heart, the pulsing edges of the world blanket the scene in white flashes

He's back in the bathroom, bare-ass naked, sweat speckled over his face. With his hands loosely holding onto the curves of a porcelain sink...Someone's knocking on the door. He shuts off the shower.

Lilith: *through the door,* Your mother just called, sweetheart. Says she needs you to help her with something.
Abe: *wiping face with the grey towel,* Oh yea?

Lilith: She needs you to help her find Enosh—He ran away. Could you check up on Sammy?
Abe: *sighs, nodding,* I'll get right on it.

Abe slips on his clothes, splashes some water over his face to work at the wild look in his eyes, and folds the grey towel back under the sink. As he makes his way out, he stops on a dime, with his hand on the doorknob.

Out of the corner of his eye, he sees it. Sticking out of the trash bin—He digs a hand in, pulling out from a pile of tissues and wrappers, a white and blue stick.

A burning red plus sign at one end.

The Curse of Heraclitus
I am in the river,
and out of it,
I am the same,
and the opposite,

I am a mountain in the distance,
and a pebble underfoot,

I am the same,
and the opposite,
I am the world,
and I am none of it.

End of Part Two:
Tender Kisses of Boiling Oil

The Curse of Orpheus
SEE HIM LIVE!
singing to the love of his life.
    Silencer of Sirens,
    Bester of Muses,
    Charmer of Stones,

    Singer of singers,
    Dancer of dancers,
    Artist of artists,

    all in his steps,
    hear his cursed lament,
    from deep below—from within,

    whispered warning at your heart,
    stop, stop, you fools,
    beware,beware
    thehand,
    of him that holds us—
    The Wealthy God.
    Owner of men;
    Owner of all;
    Owner of end;
    beware!
    beware,
    be...ware...
    be...
    but you do not hear him sing.

Not until you arrive.
SEE HIM LIVE!
singing to the love of his life.
IN THE LAND OF DEAD MUSIC

03:01 *Roaring Cathedral of Forgotten Angels*

Inside of a studio apartment on the lower east side, a phone rings, and goes unanswered. There are angels painted on these walls; Around the ceiling are a ring of angels, sounding off trumpets to the glory of a sun rising in distance behind them, soft clouds draped around their flowing purple and white robes. At their feet, stretching the rest of the room are rows and rows of candle bearers, holding lit candles from their chests as torches, mouths agape in siren's song. They have the brightest faces—bordering those trumpet players—but their feet are torn off, twisting their song into a cacophonous wail, moaned into an empty room. Their laments bouncing off of one another, in an unheard melody.

They've been here for some time, that much is obvious. Their rosy cheeks are all torn up, as if the tears they couldn't form from acrylics, instead tore themselves across those bright faces, in a series of peeling cracks. The sunset is half-white and faded, the robes are sullen with mothballs, dust, black spots. Discarded trash, beer bottles, used up blunts, and cigarette stubs have crept to the lower hem of the room. But if you looked at these walls long enough, you wouldn't see any change at all.

The smell of sour beer hangs on cool air, scented with bong hits of mornings past. A bed at the heart of the room is a mess of turned over sheets and drawings, all crumpled up, scratched over black. A shut closet holds a sparse assortment of clothes over a bag full of old paint brushes and cans of acrylics that might've fixed the forgotten angels, if not cast aside all the same. There's a bathroom off to the side. Except for a beaten up fridge shoved into a corner beside a microwave, coffee maker, and dormant stove, the only remaining piece of furniture is a worn and unsavory beige sofa.

The only sunlight entering the room is blocked by a set of thick metal bars, built into a black gate over the window. Behind it rests the rigid shoulders of a fire escape, so old that his green-brown skin has begun to shed. Behind him is one tower of bricks and cement, followed by another, and another, and on and on like this, until the only light coming between these bars is so thin and tired, that it could be drowned out by a half-dead lightbulb.

Enosh sits on the sofa, reading quietly. While Sam stands in the kitchen, stretching the strain from his arms and shoulders, topless.

Sam: *scratches his face, glancing at the unlocked gate, gears turning in reverse,* Were you playing out on the firescape?
Enosh: I wasn't.
Sam: What were you doing out there, then?
Enosh: Just some morning reading. *book held in hand,* A view's always nice to have—I like watching it all so up close.

Sam: What's out there worth watching?
Enosh: *shrugs,* All kinds of stuff. *counts off the fingers of his free hand,* There's the trains rushing across town, all the folks, the cars, the sound of it all, and the smell is something sour, but everything else is something else.
Sam: *nods, looking round the room.* Right, right, just stay the hell off the firescape. You can get hurt messing around out there. *spots something on the mess of his bed.*
Enosh: *continues,* and there's a dog that sticks around all the time. Real nice, grey and black, I named 'em Curiosity.
Sam: *picks up a cigarette and lighter,* Don't go naming those alley dogs.
Enosh: *furrows brows, gears not catching,* Why can't I name them?
Sam: Because they're sick.
Enosh: *shrinks into the sofa,* Are you sure?
Sam: Yep.
Enosh: Curiosity doesn't look sick to me. He was real calm, and sweet.

> **Sam:** That's how they all start
> out. Then they get some rabies in
> 'em, and gotta get put down
> sooner or later, *puffs his cigarette,*
> they get hit by cars, too. All day.
> **Enosh:** He looks old enough to
> know a car coming his direction.

Sam: *shrugs,* You never know when the right car'll come along. *grins wryly to the drywall,* Hell, maybe a good end of a Ford is just what he wants, huh? He might damn well starve otherwise. Some old dogs, they just need to be put down, can't go on without *feeling it,* know what I mean? Every day, every night, to the hour, to the minute, every kick to the ass and pinch in the stomach. Some dogs would rather feel nothing, after a second, then feel it all, all the time. You get what I mean? *finally sees his son, uncomfortably shifting on the sofa,*

> **Enosh:** *thinks a moment, staring
> into his book,* All he needs is some
> decent place, someone to care for
> him. *thinks a moment,* John 10:03
> to 4. That's what Pa'd say.

Sam: *shrugs,* Maybe. *puffs cigarette, letting the smoke sit in his mouth, looking about the room. eyes passing over the trash and the cracked up angels, over broken up walls, their torn up legs, the shit all over his bed.*
breathes out the smoke mucking up his tongue, You sure you wanna hang around a place like this?

> **Enosh:** *closes book over thumb,*
> What do you mean?

Sam: Maybe I should take you back—before anything I regret happens to you.
Enosh: You're not taking me back.
Sam: *dashes cigarette,* How're you so sure this is what you want?
Enosh: I need this.
Sam: *chuckles,* Hell—if I knew what I needed at fourteen.
Enosh: *almost speaks,*
Sam: *puts a hand up,* Tell you what. Give me one good reason you need to stay, and you stay. *looks around with disgust,* Cause I know damn well there ain't nothing worth while dying between these walls.
Enosh: *lets his gears turn,* I have a future here.
Sam: *sucks teeth, pouring black coffee into a mug,* We've all got a future. Here—there—anyplace. Whether you like it or not, like a chronic disease, *thinks a moment,* or taxes.
Enosh: I'll get beat on, if I go back home.
Sam: Boys here'll beat your ass up and down the block. What else you got?

Enosh: There's no money back home.

Sam: *raises an eyebrow, dumping an unhealthy amount of sugar in his coffee,* Look at this place—You think I can help you with that? Hell. I owe twice what I got.

Enosh: So, what? — What? You think I don't know what I'm getting into? *grips book with white knuckles,* That I'm just some kid on the run, cause I don't know how good I had it?

Sam: *looks the flustered boy up and down, swirling a spoon in his coffee,* Uh-huh.

Enosh: *points to the Angels,* You painted those, didn't you?

Sam: *purses lips into his cup of coffee,* Yea.

Enosh: *stands up, pacinging toward Sam,* I know that, because it's just like the church back home, Pa said you painted it. Every Sunday I'd look up and see something so beautiful that I didn't even want to pray. Just to look at it and wonder, who on Earth under Heaven could paint something so beautiful. *opens his novel up, plucking the bookmark from its spine,* Is this all you wanted to be? *flicks the bookmark at Sam, letting it fall to the floor,* Is that what you left Pa for?

Sam stares down at the business card at his feet. Looking over the hot, red snake wrapped around the thorns of a rose stem. A fluid script over the top reading, *Rose Tattoo Parlor and Piercings*. His own name, number, and address branded at the snake's tail, pierced by the rose's tip, through the '*a*'.

He looks up at the Angels, with shame painted in the shadows creasing his face. All rotting in disrepair and cracked agony. After taking it in for a few painful moments, he finally meets Enosh's eyes.

Sam: I wanted more.
Enosh: You wanted to be *somebody*! I want to be *somebody*! *tears up, walking up to his Uncle,* All I ever get is put in my place, goddamn it! I have a right to decide where that is! I got a right to own my life!
Sam: *exhales, nodding,* Alright, kid...alright, you've got someone you wanna be, then?
Enosh: *straightens up, wiping his face,* yea.
Sam: *kneels down, putting a hand on his shoulder,* Who's that, then?
Enosh: *thinks a moment,* I read all these books, and I write all this stuff down. I think, because I wanna be like Pa.
Sam: *nods,* How do you imagine?
Enosh: *takes a few breaths to make his shoulders broad. Locking them in place to make his voice steady, holding it at the right volume,* When he spoke, he knew what he

was saying. He could tell you what you needed to know, even if it wasn't what you wanted to know, and that's what made him what he was. It's what made him what I want to be.

Sam: and what's that?

Enosh: A shepherd of lost dogs.

03:02 *Quiet Cell on the Upper East Side*

These things own her like the sky owns Atlas—These work-weighed walls pressing on her temples that held her in place, every day—Oh so important numbers and names that shamed her every resting hour—Emboldened red deadlines, watching her every move and judging every minute her eyes were shut—A whole apartment on her temples and enough paperwork to smother her. So that she never moves, never stops, never sleeps. These things own her like the sky owns Atlas.

Janice carries a quiet cell on the upper east side in the back of her mind. Even if she isn't seated in that chair, typing away at that desk, or sleeping in that empty bed, she always feels that pressure on her temples.

Even as she knocks on the door to Sam's apartment.

In a few seconds the door swings open. A boy stands in the doorway, wearing nothing but a baggy pair of jeans, no belt, and a poncho in the form of an oversized red pinstripe button-up. His eyes look Janice over like he's looking at an old photograph, trying to figure out what these features amount to. Sofar as who this is, and why they're there.

Enosh: You're real pretty. Are you dating my Uncle?
Janice: *almost to herself,* Enosh?
Enosh: *smiles,* That's me.

The walls get lighter with the smile spreading on her face
Janice: Sammy's your Uncle?
Enosh: *nods.*
Janice: Is he home?
Enosh: He should be, pretty soon. He left for work this morning. *steps from the doorway, inviting her in, 'Badass' inscribed over the shirt's back, in red lace.* You can wait with me until he gets home, if you like.
Janice: *stands at the doorway,* No one taught you to not to let in strangers?
Enosh: *shrugs, sitting on the couch,* He said to lock out any muscly guys asking for money, *looks her up and down,* I don't think you're hiding any muscles, are you?
Janice: No, I'm not.
Enosh: Then we're square. *pulls a book out from under the couch, begins reading.*
Janice: *steps into the apartment,* Do you know when he'll be getting back?
Enosh: He said he'd be back after dark. Should be pretty soon, seeing as it's been dark a while now.

Janice: *nods, shutting the door,* Then I'll watch you until he gets back.
Enosh: *chuckles,* Watch me?
Janice: I can't believe he left you on your own. *thinks a moment,* On second thought, I wish I couldn't believe it.
Enosh: I don't need to be watched.
Janice: *walks over to the fridge, opening it up,* Doesn't he think a kid like you could get hurt, left alone like you are?
Enosh: *goes on reading his book,* Lady, I don't even know your name.
Janice: *looks through the interior of the beaten up fridge,* It's Janice. You can call me Janice.
Enosh: Alright, Janice. I'm my own man, now. Understand?
Janice: *chuckles,* That's a stretch.
Enosh: I am too, Sam said so.
Janice: *shakes her head,* Does he eat anything other than hot pockets and beer? I mean seriously, *shuts the fridge,* have you eaten?
Enosh: *thinks a moment,* I can make my own food.

Janice: So you've eaten, then?
Enosh: I don't see how that's any of your business.
Janice: That's a no, *starts making a few hot pockets, pushing them into the microwave, mumbling complaints, stopping to watch Enosh read,* What's that book?
Enosh: The Importance of Being Ernest.
Janice: *nods,* Oscar Wilde, he's a good one.
Enosh: *looks up to the woman,* You've read it.
Janice: I wrote a paper on it my freshman year of college. *smiles,* I love his wit.
Enosh: *beams,* It's great.
Janice: The best.
Enosh: It's not the best part though.
Janice: *pulls the hot pockets from the microwave,* What do you think the best part is?
Enosh: The lies.
Janice: *furrows brows,* What about the lies?
Enosh: *shrugs,* There's just something about it, about being someone else because you feel

like you're not up to snuff. I can feel it, I understand it.
Janice: *thinks a moment,* So it's okay to pretend to be someone else then, to lie?
Enosh: If it gets you what you want, and doesn't really hurt nobody, I think so.
Janice: *nods thoughtfully, handing Enosh a plate,* Eat your hot pockets.
Enosh: *closes the book over his thumb, taking the plate in one hand, feeling the grumble in his stomach,* Thank you.
Janice: *sits on the sofa, feeling some sheets folded over the armrest,* Do you sleep on this?
Enosh: *nods, popping pockets in mouth.*
Janice: You're not just one of his friends crashing for the weekend, you need a real bed.
Enosh: *shrugs,* my old bed was pretty stiff.
Janice: Stiff?
Enosh: I had to hide my books from Ma, *pops another pocket in mouth,* so I cut the bed open and filled it all up with what I could slip from the library.

Janice: *smirks, shaking head,* What a rebel.
Enosh: *grins,* Mhm.
Janice: So you like to read then?

A key slides into the door

Sam walks through the doorway, tired behind his aviators, wearing a blue dragon jacket, bags of groceries and clothes held in both hands. The blood drains from his face once Janice's eyes fall on him.
Enosh: Hey Sam, this pretty woman came looking for you. Her name's—
Sam: I know her name. *puts the bags down,* Go play on the firescape.
Enosh: But you said—
Sam: Now.
The walls press down hard with the look in her eyes

03:03 *Saints and Unaddressed Letters*

There's a short intermission. Sam and Janice holding their lines, until Enosh finishes changing into new clothes. Only after locking the gate shut, does Sam throw off his aviators and jacket, to have a beer from the fridge—Janice watching him, half curious, half mad-as-hell.

Sam: *kicks shoes off, collapsing into the mess of his bed, back first, beer held in hand,* Are you here?
Janice: Yes. I'm here.
Sam: *glides the beer's chilled lip over his,* You sure? *takes a long stinging drink,* Cause I'm not.
Janice: We need to talk.
Sam: *sucks teeth, eyes glazed over,* I said you're not here. I'm not here. Leave a message on your way out.
Janice: *seeing him through slitted eyes,* Are you fucked up?
Sam: *closes eyes, rolling over sheets, in a sing-song,* never came home, we never came home, she never came home,
Janice: *walks over to the sink, turning on the fauset,*
Sam: and I'm losing, lost, losing, lost, losing…time, love, time,
Janice: *walks over with a bucket in her hands,*

Sam: *whispers,* and now the next night is stealing my girl away.
Janice: *empties a bucket of water over his face,*
Sam: *bolts up-right, beer still in hand, wiping water off his face,* Alright. *dries face on sheets.* Alright, alright...You're here...I'm not fucked up.
Janice: Are you on anything?
Sam: *shakes head, wiping droplets from his bottle,* Just a couple night caps.
Janice: Good, *puts the bucket down,* now we can talk.
Sam: About what?
Janice: *eyes digging into him,* Enosh.
Sam: *gears catch, turning in reverse,* Oh, right, right. What about him?
Janice: That poor boy needs a home.
Sam: He's got a home.
Janice: Oh really?
Sam: *stands, squaring up his shoulders,* That's right.
Janice: Sleeping on a beaten up couch?
Sam: I'm working on that.
Janice: Dressed in your clothes?
Sam: That too.

Janice: Reeking of your damn cigarettes.
Sam: *shrugs,* You know I smoke.
Janice: *rubs her temples, pressure growing.*
her head is an underwater mine, jabbed by a stick with every dumb excuse that leaves Sam's lips, Have you at least put him in school?
Sam: *scratches face,* Yea...
Janice: Great. Where's he zoned into?
Sam: *snaps fingers, a goshdarnit look painted on his face,* I was just about to get that straightened out before you stopped by.
Janice: *crosses arms,* You sure about that?
Sam: *loops an arm over her shoulder,* Would I lie to you?
Janice: *coldly pinches his middle finger between her thumb and index, tossing his arm off of her, like she would a dead rat,* Nothing's stopped you before.
Sam: *puts hands up in mock surrender,* I'm as honest as a saint.
Janice: You haven't even tried to put him in school, have you?
Sam: *drops his charade,* First thing in the morning I'll have the

zoned school squared away, to finish it all up.

Janice: *pinches the bridge of her nose, shutting eyes,* His zoned school is St. Jerome, off 145st. It's literally the first thing you need to know to get him into public school.

Sam: *grins,* That saves me some work.

Janice: You'd know that if you gave a damn.

Sam: I give a damn.

Janice: Are we talking about drugs, bitches, or beer? Because you can't mean that the way you've been "raising" this child is giving any kind of a damn.

I never know how to start these.

I can't remember the last time I wrote one, but I feel like it was too long ago. This might be the best time to get this done. Seeing as there's been a lot of changes, a lot of new developments, a lot of exciting things. I know you're watching me, so updating you on these things feels unnecessary. Let me just tell you what I feel, in case heaven doesn't have the kind of view that can see people's hearts.

Part of me is scared. Part of me is really excited. They might be the same part now that I'm sitting down to think about it. These metal steps get pretty cold at night. But the sky's so pretty. There aren't any stars, not like back home. Though I don't think this place needs them. There's enough light here to drown them out.

I feel like you're both pretty close, just watching it all by my side.

That reminds me, I've been watching this dog. He feels so familiar. Like I've seen him in a dream or some distant memory. I'd like to think that, if we were all together, we'd have a dog, just like him. A yard too, and a couple of summer days. That'd be everything: Us—all together.

Sam: *chokes up the neck of the bottle,* You're one to talk.
Janice: What'd you say?
Sam: We're in the same boat when it comes to raising this kid, sweetheart.
Janice: *presses a finger to his chest,* What'd you ever do for him, jackass?
Sam: I took him from the sticks, I left him with my folks. *drinks,* That's a better start than we could've given him.
Janice: You mean better than *you* could've given him. You're such a self-centered prick, you know that? Who the hell do you think called me?

Sam: *forces a cocky grin,* Alright, you got me there, I can't pick up a phone. I'll give Ma a call as soon as you head out.
Janice: *presses harder,* Who do you think paid for his clothes, his food, his books, his toys, his diapers?
Sam: Janice—
Janice: *hardens her tone,* I sent more money for him than I had to *eat* most nights—Your parents never spent a cent on my own Son that I didn't send them. That's what being a parent is—It's nights so long that it aches to stay awake; Its dying, every day, until your son gets the life *he* deserves—It's making sure he's got clothes to wear, that fit, a real bed, to sleep in, and actual food, to eat.
It's work, a lot of work, but I made sure of all of it—While you were eating up what was left of a decent man. *jabs finger,* With the drugs, *jabs finger,* with the sex, *jabs finger,* with all the *fucking* bravado—God, just all of your-your fucking *bullshit*.
Sam: *chokes the bottle's neck with white knuckles,* Janice—
Janice: *tears up,* That's *my* son. You hear me, mine, and he's nothing like you, not anymore—
A half-empty beer bottle crashes against the wall

Somewhere in this city, there's bound to be a spot where we could've lived.

I just know it.

03:04 *Curiosity and Coming to Light*

Enosh sits on the peeling shoulders of the fire escape that hangs off of Uncle Sam's window. Glad to be so close to something hundreds of miles past his fingertips, not so many nights ago.

Taking it all in with a breath, he sees a starless night blanketing countless sleepless windows, alongside the luminescent face of a crescent moon washing its white glow on floating towers and busy streets, traffic jams and passers-by, headlights and taillights, lovers and lonely drunks, strays, runaways, crackheads, cats, dogs, rats, and all of it. Rushing by each other, toward a morning that never comes.

Because if the sun itself—with all God's divinity in palm—had come crashing down to man, it would have been in this city—This city that never darkens—This city that never sleeps—This city that never dies. As long as rats gorge themselves on scraps and sheeps sty in massive towers of bright, sleepless, and undying windows—They'll all look out at a starless night.

Enosh isn't surprised when Curiosity barks up at him from the alley. In fact, he pulls out the hot pockets he'd been saving for the hungry pup. Dropping them one by one. He does his best to keep them out of the trash and grit—though Curiosity could care less.

> **Enosh:** *watching her eat,* I knew you didn't have rabies, no sick dog would eat hot pockets like that. You're just hungry, *thinks a*

moment, frowning, cold and
hungry.
Curiosity *turns her honey-brown eyes up, wet tongue lapping warm sauce from her snout.*
　Enosh: *searches pockets,* Lemme see if I've got any more. *pulls out a last pocket,* I wish I had more for you.
Curiosity *whines up at him, bouncing on her hind legs, trying to jump the distance between them.*
　Enosh: *drops the last pocket down to the anxious stray. watching her chew it up, he folds up the unaddressed letter he'd written a few minutes ago.* Bon-apetit.

While sliding the letter into his back pocket, he hears the sound of glass breaking from the inside of Uncle Sam's apartment. It's followed by the familiar wet sound of a smack across the face. After a few moments of quiet shock, he cautiously makes his way down the steps to get a better view of what's happening between the bars of Uncle Sam's window.

　He sees Janice sitting on the couch, whispering words to Sam, who rests his head on her lap. His body shaking in the subtle way that houses do when they get old enough to collapse.
　Janice: *whispers,* It's okay, it's okay, let it all out.
　Sam: *mumbles into her lap.*
　Janice: What was that?
　Sam: *says it again and again,*

Janice: *moving fingers through his hair,* I can't understand a word you're saying.
Sam: *raises his head,* I died. I died with Clara.
Enosh: *brushes a hand over the letter,*
Janice: *pauses, softening,* You can't keep hurting yourself, it was out of your control.
Sam: *drops face to side,* I died with Clara, I died with Clara, I died that night, and it's my own damn fault.
Enosh: *gears starting to turn,* no.
Janice: There's nothing you could've done, *smooths out the reddened skin on his cheek, feeling these words sit on her tongue for the past decade,* It was dark out, there was rain on the road, and when it came down to that turn...Sammy, it could've happened to anyone.
Sam: *mumbles,* it should've been me.
Enosh: *holds tight to the letter, his palm burning up*

There's a knock at the door

Knocker: *through the door,* Damn it Sam—I know your phone's not broken! Open the damned door!

Both Sam and Janice get up to peep through the door, after a moment of whispers between them, Sam suddenly takes her by the hand. He moves to kiss her—she pulls back. Ending the moment with a slight and deliberate shake of the head. Following the silence and stillness that settles in the space of a dying moment, they part ways. Sam slips into the bathroom. Janice begins opening the door.

The door opens to Uncle Abraham

Janice: He's not here.
Abe: *furrows brows,* Janice...what're you doing here?
Janice: Ma called me, same as you, right?
Abe: *fiddles with a few things in his jacket pocket,* Right. *combs a hand through the back of his hair,* So he's not here?
Janice: *feigns deep thought,* He could be anywhere. You know him, always getting into some kind of trouble—he could be in any bar, back alley, or whore house within driving distance by

now. *pauses, earnestly concerned,* I just hope Enosh is okay.
Abe: *nods,* I've been keeping him in my prayers.
Janice: Thank you, that's very kind of you. *begins closing the door behind her,* I'll tell you if he turns up any time soon.
Abe: *stops the door from closing,* Mind if I just take a look around, first?
Janice: I already took—
Abe: *pushes through, into the apartment,* I won't take more than a minute.

Taking his first steps into the roaring cathedral, Abraham's eyes pass over all the trash and broken glass without a second thought. He sees the specks of water mingling with droplets of beer, over the cracked up and painted faces of the Angels, and thinks nothing of it. There's a set of wet spots, one on the bed, the other by the sofa.

It all seemed so typical for his brother, a mess, nothing more, nothing less, and he'd looked long enough to see no difference. If he had—truly—been looking for Enosh, he might've seen him slipping out of the window's barred frame as soon as he walked into the room.

But he was too busy fiddling with the contents of his pocket.

Abe: *sucks teeth, looking through the room for something lost.*
Janice: *crosses her arms in the doorway,* It's getting late.
Abe: I'm almost done, *picks a scratched up page from Sam's bed, looking at it,* Jesus Christ.
Janice: I've gotta get going. I know you two aren't on the best terms, and I'd rather not have Enosh in the middle of some family feud turned sunday night brawl because you happened to be snooping through his stuff when he gets home.
Abe: *puts the page down,* Alright, alright. *picks up one of the business cards,* Just let me know if you see him.

The Door Closes

03:05 *Forgotten Angels and Lost Dogs*

Enosh hangs off the room's window, dropping in with Curiosity's barks and whines behind him. A cool wind blows through an empty room of motionless things. While Angels in wait watch him enter the scene, choked up with prophecy.

The room is quiet but not peaceful, like it rests in the wake of a raging storm—a moment past. Broken glass cracks under the soles of his sneakers. A sour smell stinging his nose. For the first time, Enosh seriously looks over the room. The beer soaked into the wall and the Angels watching over him.

He imagines Sam sitting in this room, with a brush in hand, night after night—touching every delicate stroke of blush on those ruined cheeks.

He imagines Sam wasting away, with a cigarette in hand. Losing piece after piece of himself, night after night, year after year, until all that's left is a painted face on a broken man—he could see that now.

> **Enosh:** *knocks on the bathroom door,* The pretty woman's gone...hey, can we talk?

Water breaks

> **Sam:** Not right now.
> **Enosh:** Okay...It's getting pretty late.
> **Sam:** Wanna get some sleep?

Enosh: No, no, I'm not if you're not.
Sam: Get to sleep, *pauses,* Janice is getting you in school tomorrow.
Enosh: That's great. I uhm, I just think you've been in there a long while. *pauses,* Are you okay?
Sam: *sighs,* Yea, yea. Listen...kid, Janice is gonna help take care of you from now on, understand? If I'm not around, she'll be the one you go to for anything, got that?
Enosh: *nods,* Yea.
Sam: Good. Now get some sleep.
Enosh: Alright. *backs away, pacing toward the couch,*

Water sinks

Mid-step, a memory crosses his mind.

His fingers find their way over to Sam's bed, leafing through the pages scattered over it, they suck the breath from Enosh's chest. He sits on the bed, flipping through drawings and messages poured out on page after damp page.

Some of them are illustrations of Sam's suicide. One is of his caricatured head through a noose, with devil horns on his temples, and countless *'ha!'*s smothering the air around his face.

Some pages have pictures of him beside friends he's lost, with the words *'snake'* or *'asshole'* next to their faces, small passages addressed to them underneath each one. There were so many pictures, so many passages—explaining how they'd *'fucked him'*—with money, with lies, with just leaving.

Some were messages written in jagged script, made to be self-addressed letters. One page depicts an open jar of pills spilling over a counter—All around it, written over and over, are jagged letters spelling out *'do it' 'do it' 'fucking coward' 'you fucking pussy'*. Enosh almost rushes to knock on the door, but he stops to think—the gears in his head turning.

Instead, he walks over to the closet, moves all of the smoke-drenched clothes, and finally sees what he's after, in the very back of the compartment.

It takes him a moment to check the expiration date, before he grabs as much as he can. With a huge grin on his face as he takes out can after can and brush after brush and a few beaten up aprons, out into the apartment. He doesn't waste any time, he takes one look around, puts on an apron, and gets to work.

When Sam steps out of the bathroom, he sees his son, sitting in a corner of the room swept clean of trash, glass, and wrappers—apron around waist, brush in hand, painting some feet on a forgotten Angel.

He stands there for a minute, some words catching in his mouth as he walks over with a smile blossoming on his face.

Sam: *stops over his son's shoulder,* You're not holding the brush like you should.
Enosh: *shrugs,* I've never painted before.
Sam: You're not half bad. *squats down, picking up a brush,* You have to make your strokes light, *demonstrates,* like this.
Enosh: *follows suit, raising an eyebrow for confirmation from the master.*
Sam: *nods,* Good, just like that. *puts down his brush,* try not to make your strokes too long, *puts a hand over his son's, molding the fingers into form, and pushing them to make the right strokes,* like this.
Enosh: *nods,* I see, *thinks a moment,* could I watch you do it for a while?
Sam: *grins,* It's been a long time since I've sat down to—
Enosh: Please, *offers his brush,*
Sam: *looks between his son's eyes and the spark of color at the tip of the brush,* Okay. I'll take over for a couple minutes.
Enosh: *smiles, passing the brush to his Uncle, watching the color come into his face.*

They sit there for the rest of the night, so late that they stop in the morning. Playing Uncle Sam's radio to pass the time, joking the hours away, until their tired enough to sleep halfway into day.

Sam: *washing his hands in the sink,* That dog you mentioned, *thinks a moment,* Clarity?
Enosh: *corrects,* Curiosity.
Sam: Yea, that one. If you see it again, bring it inside.
Enosh: *beams,* Are you kidding?
Sam: Don't get too excited, *shuts lights,* you're house-training the mut.

When morning comes, it doesn't drip through the slits of a gate. It pours in from an open window and washes over a room full of life. With a paint coated Daedalus and Icarus asleep in a room of their design—Where new paints heal ripped and twisted roots—Where old habits are swept away for the first morning in years—Where Angels rest in wait of resurrection.

Sam's radio plays that morning,
The Roaring Cathedral sings,
Here Comes the Sun

The Curse of Orpheus
SEE HIM LIVE!
singing to the love of his life.
    Silencer of Sirens,
    Bester of Muses,
    Charmer of Stones,

    Singer of singers,
    Dancer of dancers,
    Artist of artists,

    all in his steps,
    hear his cursed lament,
    from deep below—from within,

    whispered warning at your heart,
    stop, stop, you fools,
    beware,beware
    thehand,
    of him that holds us—
    The Wealthy God.
    Owner of men;
    Owner of all;
    Owner of end;
    beware!
    beware,
    be...ware...
    be...
    but you don't hear him sing,
    until you arrive.

SEE HIM LIVE!
singing to the love of his life.
IN THE LAND OF DEAD MUSIC

End of Part Three:
Finding Forgotten Angels

The Curse of Clytemnestra
She was pleasant,
wasn't she?
our daughter,

our daughter,
who loved
you,

our daughter,
who trusted
you,

our daughter,
who died for
you,

our daughter,
you've slaughtered
in the name of Honor,

She was pleasant—
She was pleasant!
wasn't she?

these woman's hands—
like her mother's eyes—
died out of reach
and in that reach,

silence
you.

04:01 *The Pits and Rivers*

She'd put a pit in his stomach. A sinking feeling that made him clammy, every time her eyes shifted on him in the slightest. Something so intense, that he refused to call fear; he refused to be afraid, of her, of anything. Despite that nameless pit, knotting up his stomach like car sickness, stuck in a thick coat, on a balls-hot-morning.

Sammy stands a step outside of his mother's kitchen, an attempt at the unthinkable winding his hands into tight fists. The lakehouse is full of life, so simple, so clean, so lovingly put together, like a house of cards.

He's a couple of years younger than he was, sobbing on his mother's dinner table, waiting out a Winter he couldn't see from this sunset Summer scene, bordering the most pained Fall of any year.

Ma stands over a stove, watching her seven-year-old son. Abraham Jr., a contractor, making a fort from spare bedsheets and dinner-table seats—she watches him work, trying not to burn dinner. It doesn't take her very long to catch Sammy inching his way into the room, from the corner of her eye.

Ma: *raises and eyebrow*, Yes?
Sammy: *stiffens*, Well...Ma, you know I'm not so little anymore—
Ma: Don't tell me what I know, tell me what you want.

Sam: I want to go with Clara to the carnival down the road.
Ma: *rubs a hand over her forehead,* It's Sunday.
Sammy: I know.
Ma: It's gonna rain.
Sammy: I heard on T.V.
Ma: We eat together Sundays, you know that.
Sammy: I do.

A few moments pass, Ma focusing on the stove, soft raindrops pitter pattering on the windows,

Sammy: So?
Ma: *sighs,* So what?
Sammy: *tests,* Can we go?
Ma: *waves the thought away with the smoke rising from the stovetop,* Ask your father.
Sammy: He said to ask you.
Ma: Fine, *thinks a moment,* Fine—Just don't get home too late, you can take Pa's pickup with you.
Sammy: *beams, gliding out of the room. calls from the hallway,* Thanks Mom!

Ma stands over dinner burning on her stovetop—a thick smoke slipping into her nose. She could smell that burning rice for years.
    Every time she would see Sam's face.

The streets are like rivers. They cut the city into shrinking islands. So that everybody gets gradually packed in, side by side, shifting with the tide. Nameless faces passing meaningless sounds from their mouths, like rats racing in sewer tunnels.
    Cars come and go, get stuck in traffic, become traffic, look for parking, take up parking, rotate every minute of every hour, like boats crowding loaded docks. Though there's one car that doesn't move. It's anchored outside of Sam's apartment complex. A man behind the wheel has waited here so long that he's fallen asleep. His wife had called him every couple of hours and he'd answered every time. Sometime past sunset, he wakes up and sees him.
    The man rushes over before Sam can get to his car.
    Sam: *looks down at his watch,* Junior, you're gonna make me late to work.
    Abe: This is important.
    Sam: *takes a step around the wall of a man,* Can't we do this later?
    Abe: *cuts him off,* We can't.
    Sam: *sighs,* We're in public. If we're gonna go at it, we should at least have some privacy.

Abe: *nods,* Fair enough, name a place.

Sam: *side-steps, walking past the wall,* I'm saying I don't have time for privacy, we can talk after I'm off.

Abe: *grabs him by the back of his collar,* We're talking.

Sam: *turns on him, smacking the hand away,* You gonna make me?

Abe: *sucks teeth, shaking his head,* Have it your way. *grabs him by the shirt, looping an arm around Sam's knees. lifts him up, carrying Sam into a nearby alley, despite his protests.*

Sam: What the hell is wrong with you!—Have you lost your goddamn mind!

Abe: *puts him down, losing patience,* Pipe down.

Sam: *grins,* Alright, *puts hands up in mock surrender,*

Abe: I need to know—

Sam: *blurts out,* Help! Rape! Help! Help!

Abe: *smacks Sam across the face, so hard that it almost knocks him down.*

Sam: *rubs the side of his face,* Jeezus—The hell was that for?

Abe: Am I having your bastard?
Sam: What?
Abe: *pulls out everything from his pocket, the business card from Sam's apartment, the lighter with the same symbol on it, a positive pregnancy test. shoves it all into Sam's hands,* Am I having your bastard?
Sam: What the fuck is all of this shit?
Abe: Answer me!
Sam: *looks over the pregnancy test, gears turning in reverse, they catch,* Lilith's pregnant?
Abe: Looks like it.
Sam: *looks over the rest, gears catching again,* You think I'm the father?
Abe: *stares him down,* Are you?
Sam: *slowly shakes head, tossing all of it in a dumpster,* Abraham, I'm sorry to tell you this, but your wife fucks a lot of guys—
Abe: *grabs him by the neck, pushing him up against the wall,* You little shit.

Clara's room is bright and spacious. Warm pictures hung here and there. Some of her with close friends. Some of her out on the lake with Pa. Most of them paint warm pictures of her playing with her little brother, her little bean. They're lovingly posted up against posters of her favorite bands, striking pose after pose, like they're dancing just for her. A familiar window looks over a small lake and the floating towers in the distance, along with the setting sun.

She's wearing her best clothes, a white sweater over a black *Pits and Rivers* T-shirt, a knee-length floral skirt she'll trade for jeans in the back of Pa's pickup, and some old knee-high boots that she likes just fine. Along with the grin on her lips, she'd thrown all of this on, before Sam had even left to ask permission. All she was waiting on was her brother's knock on the door to get going.

A few seconds after she takes a seat on the white sheets of her bed. As if on cue, a few light knocks tap at her door. She reaches for something hidden under her bed, but a few more knocks tap on, before a small voice freezes up her arm.

    Little Abe: *through the door,* Can I
      come too, Clarry?

She shoves it back in place under her bed before opening up the door. Her little brother stands there, looking up at her with a blanket shawled over his head and around his shoulders. His whole body swaying with excitement.

    Clara: What'd you say, bean?
    Little Abe: *smiles,* I wanna go see
      the dances and eat funnel cake,
      with you and Sammy.

Clara: *bites her bottom lip, looking over to her bed, feeling the Pits and Rivers T-shirt burning on her chest. kneels down, putting hands on his shoulders,* Baby, you can't come.
Little Abe: *furrows brows,* Why can't I come?
Clara: It's getting dark out.

Cut to:

Abe's hands wrapped around Sam's neck

Sam: *choked up,* Let go—before this—gets serious.
Abe: You made it serious.
Sam: *lets a hand fall to his waist,*
Abe: *stares burning oil into his eyes,* I've got nothing left to take—you've killed me, I'm a dead man, cause you *broke* me.

Cut to:

Little Abe looking up to his sister

Little Abe: But Ma said I could go.

Clara: *shakes head,* Pa's pickup is a two-seater, there's no room for a little dancing bean.
Little Abe: I can sit in the middle, that's what we always do.
Clara: *firms up her grip on his shoulders, whispering,* I need you to stay.
Little Abe: *whines,* But Ma said—
Clara: Are you my baby?
Little Abe: *nods, the usual grin replaced with sulking eyes.*
Clara: Then, you trust me?
Little Abe: *mumbles,* Yea.
Clara: *puts her forehead to his,* Then I need you to do me a favor and stay, tonight, okay?
Little Abe: *stays silent, shaking between his shoulders.*
Clara: I promise, I'll take you tomorrow, *smiles, brushing her nose on his,* and I'll get you *anything* you want.
Little Abe: *smiles despite himself,* Anything?
Clara: Anything.

A car honks twice

Clara: *pulls away,* That's Sam.

She dashes back into her room, and slips it into her purse before Little Abe can see

Little Abe: But—
Clara: *dashes past, planting a kiss on his cheek as she goes,* I'll see you tomorrow, baby,
Little Abe: But—
Clara: *disappearing down the stairs,* get some sleep.
Little Abe: *watches the last spot he'd seen her in the hall,* I'm you're bean.

Cut to:

The Alley

Sam: *sees stars, hands numbing as they move,* let...go.
Abe: Now—
Sam: *stabs Abe in the forearm with a switchblade, cutting a red stripe down its length.*

04:02 *Honest Lies on Injured Ears*

Abe: *cries out, pulling back, hand over his bleeding arm,* SON OF A BITCH!
Sam: *drops to the floor, legs collapsing under his weight, as he coughs out breaths,* I warned you.
Abe: *presses his back against a wall, putting pressure on the wound,* You're a bastard, you know that?
Sam: *fails to stand,* If you'd let me finish, I was trying to say, 'your wife fucks a lot of guys, but I'm not one of them'
Abe: *getting light-headed,* I know you did, I know it, you can't lie to me.
Sam: *grins, leaning on a dumpster,* You know what? Fuck it—You want the truth, you're a real grown man then, yea? Big boy want to know what the truth is?
Abe: Hearing the truth from you would be a first.
Sam: When you left her alone for years, what'd you think would happen? Did you expect her to just sit and wait for you to come strutting through the front door, every morning. Every time she had a bad day, with no one to go to, or a good day to make on her own?

> **Abe:** *holds his arm with white knuckles,* I went to war—
>
> **Sam:** I was the one *she* went to! Where were you? When her father died, when she lost her job and needed a couple bucks? I gave it off a loan I haven't paid off yet, but that's not the point.
> So yea, we ended up fucking, but don't act like you did everything you could to stop that from happening. You left, she was alone, I was there. We had a fling a long time ago.
> This isn't my kid...I'm sorry.
>
> > **Abe:** *stares at the cement,* You still fucked my wife.
> >
> > **Sam:** We've all got regrets...I'm trying to be better...We're still brothers,
> >
> > **Abe:** We're not brothers.
> >
> > **Sam:** *shakes head,* You don't mean that.
> >
> > **Abe:** We haven't been brothers for years.
> >
> > **Sam:** You need to stop, before you get hurt.
> >
> > **Abe:** We stopped being brothers when Clara died.

Once they pull off the road, it doesn't take Clara very long to hop into the back of the pick-up. She starts changing, while Sammy stares at the dashboard. A few awkward minutes pass before she comes back to the front, in her change of clothes, a smirk on her lips.

Clara: *slides into the passenger seat, wringing the rain from her hair,* Better not've been peeping.

Sammy: Why am I driving?

Clara: *giggles, pulling a bottle from her purse,* Cause Ma'd kill me if I crashed the car while sipping, *deepens voice,* the Devil's hooch.

Sammy: You're not funny. Where're we even going?

Clara: *pops the bottle open,* I'll give you directions as we go. How well can you drive?

Sammy: *stares the road down, turning the ignition,* Pa takes me out every Saturday.

Clara: Great! there's a frat party at this college a ways up the road. We'll have a great time.

Sammy: Ah-huh.

Clara: *furrows brows,* What's eating you?

Sammy: I thought we were going to the carnival, *mumbles,* not an orgy.

Clara: *sucks teeth, taking a shot,* You need to loosen up. Learn how to break some rules while

you're young enough for it not to cost you, you know?
Sammy: Ah-huh.
Clara: *bites lower lip, gears snapping in place,* You know, I bet I could find some nice college girls for you.
Sammy: *grins despite himself,* Stop teasing.
Clara: I'm not. You could pass for eighteen.
Sammy: Really?
Clara: *sips,* Mhm, *pinches his cheek,* all my friends think you're a real catch.
Sammy: *waves her hand away,* Like who?
Clara: A girl's gotta have her secrets, *grins,* just know they're looking.
Sammy: *smirks, driving a little faster,*

Sam: *stands up, searching his pockets,* You don't know shit.
Abe: Then tell me what I ought to know! *barks,* Snake! Fucking Snake!
Sam: *takes out a cigarette, letting it sit between his lips.* You never see

it, but I've always tried to protect you.
Abe: Brothers protect; Snakes fuck wives.
Sam: *lights cigarette, walking over, switchblade in hand. blows smoke in his brother's drained face,* Alright. *tilts his brother's eyes up to his with the tip of his switchblade,* The truth is, she struts into my parlor every Saturday, just to find guys she can fuck. *puffs cigarette,* Brings in customers like no ad I could ever imagine.
Abe: *realizes his arms are too weak to throw a punch.*
Sam: *inches closer to his brother's face,*
Abe: *grits teeth,* Bastard.
Sam: *pats his brother on the cheek,* Save your energy, *looks around,* You'll need it to crawl to the sidewalk when we're done. You know, *puffs,* it really hurt when you mentioned Clara, *leans in, whispering smoke,* know what else hurts?
Abe: *breaks,* Sam—
Sam: I fucked Lilith on your wedding day.
Abe: *stares into Sam's eyes,* You didn't.
Sam: *grins savage,* I consummated your marriage. *puffs smoke,* I'd say she moaned like a bitch in heat,

but you ought to know what a
man fucking your wife sounds
like, by now.
Abe: *yells, charging into Sam with
his whole body, both crashing into
the opposite wall, knocking the knife
and cigarette from Sam's hands,* I've
killed real men you snake
motherfucker! *hammers a fist into
Sam's face,*
Sam: *recoils, cold-cocking his
brother in the jaw,*
Abe: *falls onto the cement, gasping
for air, bleeding out,*
Sam: We're brothers. *bends down,
taking a few breaths,* If we weren't,
I'd kill you right here. Right now.
*walks away, pulling a phone out,
dials a number,*
Sweet dreams junior—oh hello, I
need an ambulance...

He sleeps.
Argus, bleeding out in an alley.

04:03 *Curtain Call*

Rain floods the road home, it smacks thick droplets on long puddles and pours from the back of Pa's pickup. His eyes strain to see the long road between showers—Her eyes strain to stay open. Clara's drunk and Sam's buzzed. They're both tired.

Clara: *curls up in the passenger seat,* That was wild!
Sammy: *smiles, leaning into the dash, trying to carve the road from the storm,*
Clara: I know *you* had a good time.
Sammy: *shrugs,* I guess.
Clara: You think I didn't see you, getting all up close and personal on the couch. *smirks,* I see all, I am the Oracle!
Sammy: Getting wasted doesn't make you any funnier.
Clara: You know, if Ma doesn't kill us for being so late, I've got another one in about a week.
Sammy: Really?
Clara: Uh-huh, *yawns,* we could be a dynamic duo, same set up, deal?
Sammy: *grins,* Deal.

It's a small room made up of curtains as walls, with shadows passing behind them, saying things that can't catch in his ears. Like the hours that pass until he's fully awake, rather than numbly alive, they're felt but lost. He knows he'd been broken.

The air smells antiseptic and dingy; He could tell this was a hospital before the searing pain in his forearm had even registered.

The sun blankets the curtains in its golden glow, and the water drains from Abraham's ears, as he resolves to refuse any more felt but lost moments. Resolving to wake up. To be broken, but not helpless. It takes him serious effort to swing his legs over the side of the medical bed. There's a piercing pain in his wrist from the needle under his skin.

A shadow stops behind the curtain. Hearing his groans and shifting sheets, she pushes the curtain open. A young nurse puts a tray and paper-work aside.

Nurse: Oh, you don't wanna do that, hon, *gestures him back into the bed,* you need your rest.
Abraham: *follows her hands,* Where am I?
Nurse: *watches him settle back in, pleased,* L. H General, Lazarus-Hermetic, Kips Bay, *glances at the clock,* 11:00 am.
Abraham: *nods, feeling the stitches on his forearm,*

Nurse: You lost a lot of blood. *offers tray with a smile,* Eat as much as you can, gotta get your strength up, *looks him over, pleased,* Big as you are.
Abraham: Uhm, thanks. *takes the tray on his lap,*
Nurse: Was it a bar fight?
Abraham: Something like that.
Nurse: *nods,* Would you like me to get your mother?
Abraham: My mother?
Nurse: *nods,* She's been waiting all night.
Abraham: Oh.
Nurse: I can send her right in, would you like that?
Abraham: I would, *realizes her staring,* please do.
Nurse: *nods, collecting paperwork,* The name's Joanna by the way. If you like bars, maybe we could go together, sometime. *leaves Abraham with a smile,*

Curtains Close

Curtains Open
Pa walks in

His steps drag, weighed with tears held in sulking eyes.

The Night rages on mid-storm, but it's where he stands, the roof he's under, the room he's in, that soaks his dry shoulders and makes his steady hands shiver. He takes a seat, his fingers leafing through his Bible—his sinking heart's cane.

He reads for hours, looking for words to say when the air's been sucked from his chest—thoughts to hold when the unthinkable throws him—prayers to cry when he's past salvation. That's what it had always been to him, for his whole life, and it fails him in this moment.

His son wakes up in the medical bed, surrounded by curtains, his Pa reading by his feet.

Sammy: Where am I?

Pa: *flips page,* Hospital.

Sammy: *looks around,* Where's Clara?

Pa: Dead. *closes Bible, kissing it, before resting it on his lap,*

Sammy: *blinks rapidly,* What'd you say?

Pa: She's gone, son...she's, *chokes up,* She's in God's hands, now.

Sammy: *tears up, taking the pain in Pa's face, gears catching,* We...we never made it home...

Pa: *looks him in the eyes,* I won't bother asking where you were, doesn't much matter now.

Sammy: Pa, I'm so sorry—
Pa: *puts up a shaking hand,* Don't.

A moment of silence passes between them

Pa: *stands,* Not right now. *walks over to a window, watching the world drown, his tears only heard,* You're my son, you're my boy. I'll always love you...I'll always love you, but, *drops Bible on windowsill, breaking to his knees,* God made a man's heart only so strong—So please, just don't. Not tonight, not tomorrow, maybe never, but sure as Hell not right now.

Sammy: *hides between hot palms, panting quiet yells of stale breath and burning tears like a wounded animal on its deathbed,*

Pa: Junior was devastated, and your Ma...*wipes his eyes,* let me tell you something about your Ma, she hates herself. Something her Mother'd put deep inside her that eats away at her, like her soul can't take her body, understand?

Sammy: Why are you telling me this?

Pa: I'm telling you this because you need to understand what Clara meant to her; Because when we found out we were having a girl, she cried in my arms all night, cause she wanted her daughter to be everything she wasn't, *comes to Sammy's bedside, taking his hand,* and now she's been ripped from this world.

Sammy: Pa, I—

Pa: You're my son, *firms up his grip for reassurance,* but you need to understand this because...*tears up,* because your Ma's broken. Okay?
She's not here for a reason, and you need to understand that.
looks his son dead in the eyes,
This is your cross to bear.
Sammy: *takes a long look into his father's pained face,* I've never seen you like this.
Pa: I've never had my heart ripped out.

Curtains Close

Curtains Open
Ma walks in
The Sun's still bathing its glow on the curtains. Abraham's still eating his breakfast. The dingy, antiseptic air still hangs. The Night's taken its toll on her. She nearly drops into the seat at her Son's bedside. Strained eyes settling on the stitches over his forearm, she sucks her teeth, feeling every one.
Ma: How're you feeling, baby?
Abraham: *a smile graces his face,*
I'm better.
Ma: Lilith's been calling. She's real worried.
Abraham: *finishes waffles,* What'd she say?

Ma: Oh, she said she's on her way, most likely'll be here this afternoon. *looks in her purse, smiling,* She calls every couple hours to check up on you.
Abraham: *stares at breakfast,* How nice...
Ma: Mhm, *pulls out her phone,* I'll give her a call as soon as you're done eating.
Abraham: *nods, prodding his eggs,* Does she know?
Ma: Not yet.
Abraham: Could we keep it that way? *eats his eggs,*
Ma: *furrows brows, taking her son's hand,* Is something wrong?
Abraham: *chews as much as he can. because once the chewing stops, he'll have to speak,*
Ma: You can tell me anything, you know that.
Abraham: *puts down his fork and knife,* Ma, do you like Lilith?
Ma: Oh, I love her. *smiles,* I think she's a fine, fine woman, and you make a good pair, why?
Abraham: *fights the words sitting on his lips,* We're getting a divorce *is what he wanted to say. instead he says,* She's pregnant.

Ma: *beams,* That's amazing news!
Abraham: *puts tray aside,* There's just one thing.
Ma: *starts punching numbers into her phone,* I'll give her a call right now—
Abraham: *puts a shaking hand over his mother's, sulking eyes on hers,* Do you love me?
Ma: Of course I love you.
Abraham: No matter what?
Ma: No matter what.
Abraham: *sighs,* Lilith's pregnant—
Ma: I know—
Abraham: *tightens grip,* and it's not mine.

04:04 *A City of Actors*

It's been a while. Again, I'm sorry.
Everything's been moving so fast. I haven't really gotten a chance to sit down and write to the both of you. School's started, and Janice takes me out every other day.

Uncle Sam let me keep Curiosity. When we found out she was a girl, Sam started laughing (she sat to pee on the carpet, I didn't try to check). When he started laughing, I asked him, *'what's so funny'*, and he said *'Curiosity's a bitch'*.

He's at work now. He's at work most nights, and he sleeps all day. So it's been just me and Curiosity for the most part. Not that I mind. Besides, I've been going to school, whenever he's off we paint a new patch of the wall, and there's nothing wrong with having some time to read.

I've been doing a lot of thinking, dreaming about the both of you and the people you were, and what that means for me. I keep imagining this place where we could've lived. Where Curiosity could've been our dog, and I'd have whatever I felt was missing with Ma and Pa, but I can't fight the fact that I didn't really know you.

Not that I don't need you guys anymore, I think I always will, but I feel complete. Almost. With Uncle Sam, Curiosity, and Janice.

Should I feel guilty?

There are no stars. Not one in all that space of unknown blackness. Because this world was so close, so full of noise and moving parts, with no space for stars. Like the pavement is a stage, the traffic is an orchestra, and this ledge where Enosh sits is a pulpit. He watches the actors go by, under that vast black ceiling, starless and empty. Because constellations can't pay rent, and they've all been evicted.

A bag of roasted nuts take up his hand, filling his nose with a sweet smell. Curiosity sniffs it on the back of his hand, awaiting her next bit of honey-roasted goodness. While Janice sits beside him, watching the empty ceiling. He holds a few roasted nuts, letting Curiosity push her muzzle in his palm, and lap them up.

Janice: *staring up at the ceiling,* You know something?
Enosh: *scratches behind Curiosity's ear,* Yea?
Janice: I can't remember the last time I stopped to take a break, and it's not what I expected.
Enosh: What'd you expect?
Janice: *sighs, smiling soft,* I expected more stars, let's just leave it at that.
Enosh: You're looking in the wrong place, *nods to the street,* all the action's down there.

Janice: *waves the thought away,* It all looks the same after a while. *yawns,* You get tired of it.
Enosh: Don't stars always look the same?
Janice: Stars don't keep me stuck in traffic.
Enosh: They hold up the day, *eats another handful,* gets here sooner without 'em.
Janice: *smirks, nudging him,* Who said I want day to come? Is being with me really that bad?
Enosh: *shakes head,* This is nice. *thinks a moment,* I just feel like it's hard to find bright spots in the Night, dark as it is.
Janice: *nods,* You know something else about stars?
Enosh: *gives Curiosity the rest of the bag, wiping hands on his jeans,* What else?
Janice: People used to believe the stars were Angels, *smiles,* guardians, watching over all of us.
Enosh: No Angels in the city then?
Janice: *shrugs,* I think you see them if you look hard enough.

Enosh: *looks up,* There's one right there. *points.*
Janice: *follows his finger,* You made that look easy.
Enosh: *shrugs,* It's always there, hard to catch at first, but I've been out here pretty often.
Janice: *smiles,* Lucky you. *stares up at the lone star,* Looks like you've got one looking out for you, *sighs,* in this heaven of our misery.
Enosh: *furrows brows, gears catching,* William Blake?
Janice: *nods, speaking through a proud smile,* That's right, very sharp.
Enosh: Pa loved those poems.
Janice: I never took him for the type.
Enosh: *furrows brows,* You knew Pa?
Janice: Yea, of course.
Enosh: How?
Janice: *chuckles,* We didn't really get off on the right foot. *smooths out her hair,* You see, Sam and I went to church together. *eyes softening,* You know, he painted it back then. It was *gorgeous,* like a little Sistine Chapel—I just *had* to meet him. God, he was so, *pauses,* so *much.* So much more than he is now—Completely different.

Enosh: Were you the one he took into the confessional?
Janice: *sighs,* No, *watches traffic pass,* I was the one he took up to his room.
Enosh: Oh...
Janice: *glances at her watch,* Wanna know something else?
Enosh: Sure.
Janice: *gets up, looking to the empty ceiling,* Some people don't change. Not really. *sighs,* We look back on Yesterday, and think they're the people we want see Today. Remember that Enosh, *puts her jacket on,* save yourself some disappointment.
Enosh: You're leaving?
Janice: *puts sad eyes on him,* Yea. *glances back down at her watch,* I've got work early tomorrow morning.
Enosh: *stands,* Are you coming tomorrow?
Janice: *hugs him,* I'll try my best.
Enosh: I'll hold you to that.

For a few moments the roof is theirs. The only sound is that of idling traffic, and passing arguments in the distance, that seem to get farther and farther away with each passing second. It feels isolated, at peace, until Janice notices something in his back pocket.

Janice: What's that?
Enosh: *pulls away,* What's what?

Janice: That paper in your back pocket.
Enosh: It's...it's a letter.
Janice: A letter to who?
Enosh: *looks away...*my parents.
Janice: *looks on him with soft eyes,* would you mind if I read it?
Enosh: *thinks a moment,* Alright. *hands it to her,*
Janice: *reads it over, breathing in deep, trying not to cry,*
Enosh: Are you okay?
Janice: *forces a smile,* Yea. *takes a shaky breath to steady herself,* How long have you been writing these?
Enosh: Long as I can remember.
Janice: And you always write to your parents?
Enosh: *mhms,*
Janice: Can I ask you something?
Enosh: Anything.
Janice: When you write these letters, what do you think of your mother?
Enosh: *thinks a moment,* I talk to her sometimes. When I can't sleep, when I'm real sad, or when I've got no one to talk to. She never talks back, but, *looks up at the lone star,* I feel like I know she cares. Like she's listening and wants to tell me sweet things, and hold my head in her lap, and hush me.

Letting me know that all the bad's gotta end some time, and the sun'll rise every morning.
and I miss her, even if I never met her, or can't see her.
and I think of her, and I feel safe.

    Janice: *smiles, tearing up,*
    Enosh: *furrows brows,* Is something wrong?
    Janice: *hugs him, pressing the letter against his back,* You're a baby, you know that?
    Enosh: *awkwardly returns the embrace,*
    Janice: There's something I need to tell you, but it needs to wait...Okay?
    Enosh: Does this mean you can stay?
    Janice: *chuckles, wiping eyes,* I wish I could.

04:05 *The Lies We Spare With*

    A Night, sewn up in thread of countless stars, blankets itself over the scene. It wraps around the shoulders of still trees, resting on branches, and lulling Chimney Swifts in their nests to sleep. While hiding Nighthawks perched on high branches, on the hunt. The stars watch over this withered lakehouse, its placid lake, and the bonfire between them. They watch over Enosh and Pa, sitting together, with s'mores roasting over the bonfire.
    Stars make the scene beautiful, but the bonfire between them makes this night warm and bright. It's what staves off the wildlife. It's what keeps their hands and faces warm and toasty.

    Enosh: *whistles, looking up to the stars,* That's a sight to see, don't you think, Pa?
    Pa: *nods,* It's burning.
    Enosh: *thinks a moment,* Yea—way up in that darkness. All those stars look like they're burning.
    Pa: *chuckles,* I meant your stick, son—It's burning up.
    Enosh: *pulls a charred-over marshmallow from the bonfire's dancing hair.*
    Pa: Here, *offers his s'more in exchange for the torch in his grandson's hands,*

Enosh: *makes the trade, dancing shadows shading the shame on his face,* Thanks, Pa.
Pa: Buck up, son. *blows the torch out,* No shame in watching the heavens—just try to keep your head where your feet are while you do it.
Enosh: *nods,* I'll try.
Pa: *looks the boy over,* You're getting big now, aren't you?
Enosh: *smiles,* Yea.
Pa: *sucks teeth, scratching face.* I'm getting old, *stares up at the burning blanket.* Aren't I?
Enosh: *shrugs,* Yea.
Pa: You know, son, I won't always be around.
Enosh: *shifts uncomfortably,* I don't really like thinking 'bout it, but I know.
Pa: *nods,* I won't be gone, you know. Just...not around.
Enosh: *gears turning,* Where'll you be, then?
Pa: *sighs, mumbling,* Ain't that the question.

Enosh stares at him, expecting an answer,

Pa: *looks to his grandson,* Wanna know where I'll be?
Enosh: *nods,*
Pa: Come ere 'an I'll show you.
Enosh: *sits beside his Pa.*
Pa: *resting an arm on Enosh's shoulders, points out to the horizon, sitting on the lake,* See there?
Enosh: *squints,* I don't see much.
Pa: It's dark out now, it's hard to see. *traces a line over the horizon-line,* That's where the sun meets the water, when the days come to an end.
Enosh: *furrows brows,* You'll be there?
Pa: No, not there. But when the sun comes down, and breaks over all that water, and all you see is this burst of orange-pinkish light like the Lord's kissing the sky goodnight—*that's* where I'll be.
Enosh: *breathes out, trying to imagine it in the blackness of night he sees in its place,* Wow.
Pa: In those minutes when heaven meets Earth, and you've had your nice day in the sun, *holds him close,* and you're getting ready to wait out a cold night—I'll be there. With you, watching you, guiding you. Understand?
Enosh: *nods,* I think so.
Pa: *tears up, pressing a finger into the center of his grandson's chest,* I'll be right here, too. Right in there,

with you—every step of the way, till you come see me yourself. *kisses him on the temple,* You never forget that. Ever. Understand?
  Enosh: I won't—I promise.

   the night passes warmly for a few hours,

 Pa: *yawns,* I think I'm calling it a night.
 Enosh: *gears turning,* Wait, Pa, can I ask you something?
 Pa: Anything.
 Enosh: *thinks long on the words he can't say. trying to put them together in just the right way,* Uhm, where you said you'd be, when you're...not around?
 Pa: What about it?
 Enoh: Are my parents there?
 Pa: *pauses, looking up at the stars, watching his words,* Uhm...yea, *nods,* yea, son. They'll always be with you.
 Enosh: *thinks a moment,* Can you tell me something else?
 Pa: *sighs,* Sure. What else you need to know?
 Enosh: How'd they die?
 Pa: *stops, heart dropping,* Enosh—

Enosh: You said anything, *tears up, I need* to know.
Pa: *thinks a moment,* Alright. *nods, rubbing a palm over sorry lips, feebly trying to smear the lie about to leave them,* Your mother died in a car crash.
Enosh: *gears turning,* What was her name?
Pa: *without a second thought,* Clara.
Enosh: *nods in understanding,* What was she like?
Pa: *looks down at empty hands,* She was...everything. *closes eyes, to himself,* Everything.
Enosh: *furrows brows,* What about my dad?
Pa: *looks Enosh dead in the eyes,* He died in that crash too.

The Curse of Clytemnestra
She was pleasant,
wasn't she?
our daughter,

our daughter,
who loved
you,

our daughter,
who trusted
you,

our daughter,
who died for
you,

our daughter,
you've slaughtered
in the name of Honor,

She was pleasant—
She was pleasant!
wasn't she?

these woman's hands—
like her mother's eyes—
died out of reach
and in that reach,
silence
you.

**End of Part Four:
Ripping Stitches on Old
Wounds**

Cradle Song

Sleep, sleep, beauty bright,
Dreaming in the joys of night;
Sleep, sleep; in thy sleep
Little sorrows sit and weep.

Sweet babe, in thy face
Soft desires I can trace,
Secret joys and secret smiles,
Little pretty infant wiles.

O the cunning wiles that creep
In thy little heart asleep!
When thy little heart doth wake,
Then the dreadful night shall break.

05:01 *Of Men and Mothers*

  The withering lakehouse looks worse for wear and near death, as old houses tend to rot until torn down for new homes. Light droplets of rain pitter patter outside, soaking into a roof bogged down by decades of storms. Ugly spring peeper frogs croak their base laments, beside the forlorn high honks of snow geese—all soaked in Fall showers.
  Ma sits with her table, alone, and empty. Smoking a cigarette she dashes on the bare skin of the Sequoia tabletop. Burning ashes falling beside a heavy stack of papers, neatly put together, its top-most sheet hiding the rest behind its pale white back. Placed deliberately, down to the position of the paperclip at

the upper left corner, and the pen at its footer. Like everything personal to her, she'd handled it with care. Excessive care.

The cigarette is dashed halfway by the time Lilith gets to her front door. Ma takes her time. Letting smoke settle over her tongue, rolling a piece of hot metal in her palm. She gets up and dashes her cigarette around the tenth knock, letting another six fall before she reaches the door.

Ma: *opening the door a crack,* Hello?
Lilith: It's me, *waits,* Lilith.
Ma: *opens door,* My eyes aren't what they used to be.
Lilith: *smiles, stepping inside,* That's perfectly alright.
Ma: *walks to the kitchen,*
Lilith: *looks around,* Where's Abe?
Ma: He's doing fine. Just fine.
Lilith: Oh, no, I said—
Ma: Sit. *walks into the dining room, plate of hot food in hand,* Please.
Lilith: *takes a seat,* I'm sorry, I don't have an appetite.
Ma: *sits, putting cold eyes on her,* Who said this is for you?
Lilith: I just assumed—
Ma: Assumptions reap disappointment. *starts eating,*

A few awkward moments pass

Lilith: Is something wrong?
Ma: You tell me.
Lilith: What's that supposed to mean?
Ma: You've got ears, don't you?
Lilith: Where's Abe?
Ma: I told you: He's fine.
Lilith: *loses patience,* If he's not here, then why'd you call me?
Ma: *sucks teeth, gesturing to the pile,*
Lilith: What's that?
Ma: *digs a ring from her pocket, slamming it down on the pile,* Deliverance; Romans 6:16.
Lilith: *picks the ring up, confused. realization sucking the air from her chest.*
almost to herself, His wedding ring...
Ma: *nods, eating,*
Lilith: *flips over the top-most page of the neat pile, heart dropping, with the blood that drains from her face,* What...what the Hell is this?
Ma: *raises an eyebrow,* I'd thought you'd know how to read, *wipes hands with napkin,* sly as you are.
Lilith: *holds the paper with a shaking hand,*

Ma: See here. *gestures to the emboldened letters at the top of the page,* Says dee-vorce appli-cay-tion form.
Lilith: *turns pleading eyes on her,* Why is he doing this?
Ma: Could you please speak english.
Lilith: What?
Ma: *leaves for the kitchen,* I'm fluent in bitch, *sink runs,* not adulterous cunt.
Lilith: Can I talk to my husband?
Ma: What husband?
Lilith: Can I see Abe?
Ma: *stands in the dining room doorway, rough hands choking a washcloth, cold eyes set on her, mad-as-hell,* No.
Lilith: I'd just need a minute—
Ma: *sucks teeth,* See, there you go again, with those words I just can't understand.
Lilith: Please.
Ma: Sign the papers.
Lilith: Please!
Ma: Sign the papers! I don't speak adulterous cunt!
Lilith: *Fuck* you!
Ma: Now you're speaking my language.

Lilith: *shakes between her shoulders,* I'm sorry.
Ma: I'm not—sign the papers.
Lilith: *drops the page on the table,* Not until I see him.
Ma: You're not seeing my son. Not anymore.
Lilith: *chills over, steadying her voice with a breath,* I'm not signing.
Ma: The door's locked.
Lilith: I'll call the police.
Ma: *sits,* Test me. Whore.
Lilith: You'll go to jail.
Ma: *leans in, eyes cold as death, voice hard as stone,* I'm not my son. I'm not your mother. You're nothing to me, and I want you the fuck out of my house. You're not in kansas anymore. So best believe, if you fuck around with me, I'll mess that pretty, filthy mouth up like a good mother ought to. *picks the pen up,* Test me.

Lilith takes the pen with shaking fingers

Abraham takes his beer with a full grip

It's bright as day in the heart of manhattan, deep into night and long after sunset, but he feels awake. He feels alive. That much is seen in the difference of his face—of his eyes, settling on her.

This Irish pub is typical of any you could find dotted all across Manhattan. It's packed in, with ambient music over dozens of ongoing conversations.

One of these being held between Abraham and Joanna—the nurse he'd strolled here with, after days of hospitalization, and hours of follow-up foreplay.

    Abraham: *grins into the lip of his beer,* You look good out of scrubs.
    Joanna: You look plenty, regardless.
    Abraham: Can you blame me?
    Joanna: I can't. *looks his face over,* God. You're so young.
    Abraham: Is that a bad thing?
    Joanna: No, no, I just remember the first time I saw your chart, and I couldn't get past it. *brushes the side of his hair with her fingers,* You're too young to be a veteran.
    Abraham: *nods, raising his beer,* Amen to that.
    Joanna: Too handsome to be married.
    Abraham: *bottle burning in his hand,* You knew?
    Joanna Bit of a letdown at first.
    Abraham: *sobers,* I'm sorry. I should've—
    Joanna: Oh relax! If it bothered me, I would've told you.
    Abraham: I'm getting a divorce.
    Joanna: *chuckles,* I knew that too, if I didn't, we wouldn't be here.

Abraham: *inspects her face, waiting for answers,*
Joanna: Wanna know my secret? *leans in, whispering,* Curtains happen to be the thinnest walls.
Abraham: *nods in realization, smiling,* You're a spy, then. I knew it—explains a lot.
Joanna: What's that supposed to mean?
Abraham: You're too smart to be a Nurse, a doctor maybe, but not a Nurse.
Joanna: *chuckles,* Oh really?
Abraham: and you're pretty enough to be a model.
Joanna: *pats his shoulder,* I'm sold, Prince Charming, you can stop gushing.
Abraham: Is that so?
Joanna: *looks up into his face,* I can prove it to you.
Abraham: I'd love to see that.
Joanna: *pushes her lips up against his,*

There's something there; Something concentrated, that'd built up in the space between them. A tension; A tension that moves his arms to wrap around her waist, his hands to feel as much as they can, his lips to take up hers, his heart to beat in time with the seconds, to slow down the minutes and hold time up to where he gets as much of *this* as he can. This something he hasn't had in a long-time. And it feels good. And it feels warm.

    Abraham: That was...
    Joanna: *eyes on his lips,* Worth the wait.
    Abraham: *breathes out, pleased,* Yea.
    Joanna: *glances to the doorway,* My place, then?
    Abraham: What?
    Joanna: I would ask yours, but you have the whole divorce thing going on.
    Abraham: I know, I just...it's been so long—
    Joanna: Do you want this or not?
    Abraham: I do.
    Joanna: *smiles,* My place it is.

Abraham is led through the bar and out an open door by the hand, his eyes glazed over, a grin warming his face, the sounds of laughter and happiness in the dead of night at his back.

Hours of follow-up foreplay, years of trauma, and layers of clothes come off him in the small hours of the morning. For all of his reservations, all his fears that at that pivotal moment of the night, he might shrivel up and fail, when the moment came, he couldn't have been more prepared. For the first time, in a long time, he felt he was a man, and what's more, he had his woman. In that moment, he could see the truth. That it was never the war that had broken him, but what he came home to, that ruined him, and for the first time in a long time, he sleeps. He sleeps so well that he feels like crying tears of joy when he wakes.

His ex-wife to-be had called a few times that he couldn't be bothered with. They were as inconsequential as the time, as present as the ambient music, and as important, to him, as the clothes he left scattered across the floor.

    Because for the first time in a long time,
        he did not answer.

05:02 *Of Boys and Uncles*

An apartment on the lower east side is bright and full of life. There are Angels on these walls, Angels made up of fresh paint, drying over the old wounds of warm faces; Around the ceiling are a ring of glowing angels, roaring their trumpets in fanfare of a golden Sun that bursts at their backs. Soft clouds draped around their flowing purple and white robes. At their feet, stretching the rest of the room, are rows and rows of candle bearers, holding torches from their chests, warm-faced smiles agape in silent serenade. They've the brightest faces—bordering those trumpet players—but it's Uncle Sam's radio that fills their mouths, with the tune of *Cat's in the Cradle*.

The gate on the window stays open, for the spring breeze and sun beams that slip in with Enosh throughout the day. Curiosity idles around the apartment. A twin bed, covered in sheets of soft wool and under-drawers stuffed to the brim with books, rests in place of an old beaten up couch. The floor's swept clean, and though Sam's bed is never made, it's never piled with all those scratched up pages. It's almost too good to be true, too fresh to have dried, too bright to not have a few unspoken shadows.

Curiosity stares at the door before it opens, and Enosh walks in with a schoolbag. He makes quick work of realizing that Uncle Sam's gone, having checked his bed, and the bathroom, and the room that was the apartment. He settles into his bed, petting Curiosity while listening to the radio.

Enosh: *nods, gears catching,* That's right. Janice said they'd be going out for lunch. *sighs, looking into Curiosity's chocolate eyes,* Do you know what they've got to talk about?

Curiosity looks up at him a moment, as if contemplating some great truth, before she licks his fingers, begging more scratches behind the ear,

Enosh: *abliges,* I'll take that as a no. *thinks a moment,* It's got to do something with my folks, right? It has to...right?

Curiosity gives no answer, except for light licks on fingertips.

Enosh: *sighs, opening up a book, gears turning for the next couple hours,*

Day sinks into Night

Two voices argue out in the hall

Once Enosh recognizes the two voices as Janice and Sam, he decides to hide on the firescape, and eavesdrop for whatever parts of the conversation he could manage. The gate to the window closes behind him.

The door unlocks. The two voices hush. It opens. Sam and Janice walk in, looking around the room as Curiosity dances around Janice's legs, licking at her ankles.

Sam: *closes the door to the bathroom,* He's on the firescape, like always.

Janice: I'm not leaving without an answer.

Sam: I don't know what you wanna hear, what do you expect—

Janice: This isn't fair to Ma. He's spent his whole life with her, don't you think she wants to at least *see* him?

Sam: *scratches face,* Yea...

Janice: Why can't we just tell him? The Hell are you afraid of?

Sam: *sits on bed, looking around the room,* What if...what if he expected more?

Janice: *sits with him,* and what if he did? Would you rather lie to him, every day?

Sam: I'm good at living lies, Jane, *looks into his hands,* I'm awful at everything else, and I'm sure as Hell not what that boy needs.

Janice: What do you think he needs?

Sam: Someone like you.

Janice: *smiles,* What's that supposed to mean?

Sam: *gestures around the room,* This isn't me, this is you. I'm not warm, not like you are, I'm not reliable, *sighs,* I'm frozen hot pockets and beer, you're not.
Janice: Sam—
Sam: You gave him a bed, you were there, he likes you, the damn dog likes you. I let it in myself and it licks you first. Cause *he* likes you better.
Curiosity shrinks away with Uncle Sam's eyes on her,
   Janice: *blanketing his hand with hers,* Sam—
     Enosh touches the last letter he's written,
  stowed away in his back pocket,
Sam: You tell him. He deserves a mother like you. I could never tell him I'm his father—
Janice leans her body into him, stopped by the 'WHAT!?' that blurts out from behind the slitted gate,
  the couple looks to the gate,
    it swings open,
    Enosh drops in,
For a few moments, it's quiet. The space growing between them with every second of silence. Like a tide that pulls the tears from Enosh's eyes and creeps

them down his warm face. Like the sinking feeling that pushes Sam's face into a bath of shadows, drowning his remorseful eyes.

In a few tense moments, the space comes crashing together, snapping back in place, the silence broken with the boy's quiet words.

Enosh: *pulls the letter from pocket, looking between them,* You knew.

Sam: *stands,* Enosh...I'm sorry. I—

Enosh: *shaking his head,* You are not my father.

Janice: *stands,* Enosh, please—

Enosh: *takes the letter with both hands, crumpling the paper with the force of his fingertips,* You are not my mother.

Curiosity *shrinks into a corner, tail tucked between her legs,*

Enosh: *rips the letter apart, falling to his knees, sobbing into the scraps of his dreams,*

Janice: *kneels down, taking her son's sobbing face in her lap,*

Sam: *to himself,* I didn't want it to happen this way.

Enosh: *sobbing,* Why...why didn't you tell me?

Janice: *croons,* We loved you too much.

Sam: Mistakes have a way of piling up, Son.
Enosh: Don't call me that.
Sam: *sighs,* I knew this'd happen, *looks up at Janice,* I told you this'd happen.
Janice: *digs eyes into him,*
Sam: *looks back at Enosh,* Do you hate me, is that it?
Enosh: *shakes head,* No, no, I love you.
Sam: Then what's got you so upset.
Enosh: You can't be my father. We buried him. I was there.

05:03 *Of Daughters*

She could feel it in her bones. She didn't have very long on this Earth. An aching kept off by medication, like a rotting house on support beams, waiting to collapse in on itself mid-Winter.

So she went to see her, after decades, after lifetimes. She goes where she couldn't return, not until this moment. Because whatever damage it could do her heart, couldn't be worse than the time spent apart, not now.

A mother parks her car before her daughter's tombstone, stepping out with the sight of it burning a cold pain in her heart. The day is coming to an end with a setting sun in the distance. In time with her eyes sinking on the sight of the tombstone, weighted with the tears she refuses because she is not a crying woman, but she's had more than enough pain despite it.

She walks, weak but rigid, until she reaches the grave, until she falls on her knees and lets the plastic-wrapped flowers fall from her hand. Red petals and tears of a hollowed woman falling over hallowed land.

In the shadow of Clara's tombstone growing over the grass beside her mother, the daughter stands. Watching this mother she'd not seen in decades, in lifetimes, break at her feet.

What she'd never seen in life, she can't believe in death, and when her mother speaks, unseen to this world, she listens, in the next.

Ma: *sobs*, I'm so sorry.
Clara: I'm here cause of my mistakes—not yours.
Ma: I should've been better.
Clara: I couldn't have *had* better.
Ma: You've been gone so long.
Clara: Too long...I know you're tired.
Ma: I'm so tired.
Both: It gets harder every day—I cry every night.
Ma: I never wanted you to leave.
Clara: I never wanted you to cry.
Both: *bathed in twilight,*
 But here we are...
 and it's all my fault.
Ma: I said I'd be better...
Ma pounds the earth in defiance

—

Big Ma pounds the table in dominance

Stopping Candace at the first step of the staircase.
 It's an old house that Candace had left a lifetime ago. She's wearing a white floral dress, in a beige cardigan, with black slippers. These were her church clothes, she remembers, and she wasn't but sixteen years old. Her mother's a big woman, with thick slabs of hands that she knew like the back of her own small and dainty ones.

Big Ma's voice had a dial; An inside and an outside voice that seemed mismatched with what you'd expect from them. Her outside voice was used on the neighbors, the mailman, her gal pals, and all that said *mornin'* on any given day. Pleasant as pie—But her inside voice was used with Candace, her brother, the rats under the cupboard, and the cockroaches behind the fridge. Cold as ice, hard as a smack to the side of the head.

And they were inside, so Candace kept quiet, cause she'd been kept quiet the hard way for longer than she could remember.

> **Big Ma:** *scraping cold slitted eyes over her daughter's dress,* Well? Aren't you embarrassed?
> **Candace:** *mumbles,* 'mbarrassed 'bout what?
> **Big Ma:** *nods, sucking teeth,* You real stupid, aren't you?
> **Candace:** If you say so.
> **Big Ma:** Don't get smart with me. You know damn well what you did.
> **Candace:**...I don't.

Big Ma: *sighs,* You know you're never gonna get a husband, not a decent one, don't you? You can't clean worth a damn, you can't cook worth a damn, you don't make yourself up worth a damn, and you're dumb as a brick—I mean really, no man's got a reason to *give* a damn. *sucks teeth,* Probably end up with a drunk, or one that'll beat on you, or worse, you keep acting like this.

Candace: That's not true.
Big Ma: Don't talk back to me.
Candace: *takes a step up the stairs,*
Big Ma: Did I say you could leave?
Candace: *mumbles,* No.
Big Ma: Then why're you leaving?
Candace: I don't know.
Big Ma: *to herself, shaking head,* See. Dumb as a brick, and disrespectful too. Ain't never gonna find a good man.
Candace: What'd I do wrong?
Big Ma: *widens eyes,* You *still* don't know? You forgot your damn stockings in the house of God. Like some, *waves heavy hands,* some Slut! Some Whore!
Candace: *tears up for the last time,* I **Hate** you!

A few moments of shock pass between them

Big Ma: *blinking rapidly,* What'd you say?
Candace: I said I hate you—I fucking hate you and you're

wrong! I'll never be anything like
you!
Big Ma: *slams her hand on the
table, standing,*
Candace: *holds her ground, barking,*
I fucking dare you!
Big Ma: *freezes up in shock,*
Candace: *mad-as-hell,* You're wrong! *slams her hand on the railing,* I'm gonna find me a man, *hits again,* and he's gonna be good! *slams railing,* and he's gonna be better than every drunk deadbeat you done dragged through here since Pa died, you hear me?! And when I'm grown, *takes cardigan off,* Imma leave with him, and *never* come back—
Big Ma: *breaking,* Candy—
Candace: *throws it off,* Just so I never have to see your face again! *storms up stairs, slamming door shut,*
Big Ma:
*sinks to the floor,
mourning the death of a daughter,*
Big Ma breaks to her knees

—

Ma stands with an aching body
*mourning the death of a daughter,
shedding tears a lifetime past due,*
 Clara kneels down, sinking into the earth with the setting of the Sun, to rest with a dying twilight. She looks on at her sobbing mother, mourning into Night over the daughter she'll never see again, not in this world.
 And with the lightest kiss, light as breeze, on her mother's temple,

she says:
This is not goodbye,
this is goodnight,
and she's gone.

05:04 *Of Fathers*

It's quiet in Pa's old pickup. The tension between the two of them unbroken for half the drive, except for the sounds of night passing, out of this moment, a lifetime ago. Whatever Pa could say needed Sam's input, which he was surely not going to give. Given the numb look in his eyes, watching traffic and trees pass by his window. It was a thought that broke the silence, a thought that made Pa chuckle.

Sammy: *looks him over,* What's so funny?
Pa: *shrugs,* Nothin', it's just, every time you run away I tell your Ma to give you more chances, and every time I gotta come get you, she says to give you less.
Sammy: I don't see the joke.
Pa: *shrugs,* Truth has a way of coming out like a bad joke sometimes.
Sammy: *stares back at window,* Uh-huh.
Pa: How many times is it gonna have to be, Sammyboy? How many times?
Sammy: How many times till what?
Pa: *sighs,* Till you get your head out of, let's be honest, your very own ass.
Sammy: *shrugs, staring at the night out his window,*

Pa: This time, it's trespassing. Last week was assault, last month was a trail mix of vandalization, public intoxication, petty theft, obscenity, resisting arrest, and every time I got to call in favors to get you square—I mean really, are you *trying* to hurt your Ma's heart, mah boy?

Sammy: I don't need a lecture.

Pa: *mumbles,* You *need* Jesus.

Sammy: What's Jesus done for me lately?

Pa: *stops car,* What'd you say?

Sammy: *shrinks back, Pa's eyes on him,* I didn't say nothin' Pa, I was just rambling is all.

Pa: *sucks teeth,* That right? *thinks a moment,* Oh, so you're not satisfied breaking your Ma's heart—Noooo sirry, you gotta come after your old man too,

Sammy: That's not what I meant—

Pa: Cause you're a man now, and don't you know? The whole world's against you, even me, right? Jesus too then? Is he having you make these mistakes?

Sammy: *looks down, sobering,* I didn't mean it, Pa.

Pa: Damn right, you didn't mean it. *pulls back on the road, mumbling,*

'What has he done for me lately'—the nerve.
Sammy: *feels hot shame on his cheeks,*
Pa: *mumbles, shaking head,* 'What has Jesus done for me lately'—done lost his damn mind.
Sammy: I'm sorry.
Pa: Oh you sorry, now?
Sammy: Yes. I'm sorry.
Pa: *wraps white knuckles over the wheel,* You need to get your head out of your ass. That, or learn to use those legs God gave you. Walk out of jail your own damn self, next time—better yet, learn to pray while you wait for morning.
Sammy: I don't know what you expect.
Pa: *sighs,* I don't know either. Not anymore.
Sammy: *stares out his window,* At least you have Junior.
Pa: *relaxes grip,* Junior's a fine boy, keeps his room clean, keeps his grades straight, checks all the boxes and loves his Ma, but he'll never be you. Not in my eyes.
Sammy: *furrows brows, gears not catching,* What's that supposed to mean?
Pa: Sammyboy, you've got something in you most people

never have, and I don't think Junior ever will.
Sammy: And what's that?
Pa: Greatness. *sighs,* Wasted greatness, but greatness all the same—deep down.
Sammy: *beams,* Pa, I—
Pa: Under all the bullshit, *chuckles,* under lots, and lots of bullshit.
Sammy: *dulls,* Gee, thanks.
Pa: *chuckles,* I mean it, son. You've got something.
Sammy: What's so great about it?
Pa: *thinks a moment,* One day, you'll have kids, and if you've got all this stuff behind you, and your head where your feet are. You put all that effort you put into beautiful paintings, into them—you might just be a better man for it, better than me. *smiles, ruffling up his boy's hair,* That's what I've always wanted for you, mah boy: Greatness.

Sammy stares out into the night

Sam stares at Sammy in the mirror

Pills next to the toilet. In the dead of night. His face speckled with sweat and faucet water, torn between chronic habits and the future awaiting him out the door. Between both sides of the mirror, from that night, driving in his Pa's pickup, to this night, haunted by his words. He hasn't changed much.

He sees his younger self as clear as yesterday. Sammy sees his older self in that blurry photograph in motion that's our vision of our future. Both displeased. For different, but similar reasons.

Sam's eyes pass between the mirror and his open bottle of pills. Sammy's eyes pass between the reflection of what he is and what he might become. Sam's eyes wander to the toilet, Sammy's eyes wander to the reflection of the father at his back.

>They look back into each other's eyes.
>**Both:** I'm not you.

05:05 *Of Brothers*

Daylight pours out over the city. It bathes the nameless, faceless masses and washes over countless buildings, one of which being the bar Abraham had kept in fond memory.

Typical of most irish bars dotted across Manhattan, it looks completely different mid-day. There's a couple of regulars that enjoy their quiet drinks of the evening. They all meander about, making no conversation, except for the occasional small-talk, as they all know each other, but not very well.

No one speaks to Abraham, waiting with broad shoulders at one of the tables that'd gone missing a few nights ago. Soon enough his brother comes, walking through the doorway, a wide grin on his face, despite his desperate lack of sleep.

Abraham: *waves him over, the stab wound burning on his forearm,*
Sam: *approaches. careful, despite the confidence he's draped in,* I take it this is important? I don't think you've ever called me out for dinner, let alone a drink.
Abraham: *smiles,* It's incredibly important.
Sam: *sits,* God, I didn't know you could be so happy. *looks him over in mock concern,* Are you high?
Abraham: No. Better—

Sam: *kids,* Cause I know the right people, if you ever need to be.
Abraham: *chuckles,* No, no, I'm happy. Just happy, *sighs,* for the first time in a long time.
Sam: *raises an eyebrow,* I knew something looked different about you.
Abraham: And I've got you to thank for that.
Sam: *raises an eyebrow,* Thank me for what?
Abraham: *rolls up sleeve, exposing the stitched up wound across his forearm,* This.
Sam: I don't follow.
Abraham: It put everything in perspective, you know? *sighs, rolling sleeve down,* You get so caught up in trying to be what you're supposed to be, that you forget who you are, and that's when a good smack upside the head can really give you the push you need.
Sam: *smirks,* That, or getting sent to the hospital for losing your goddamn mind.
Abraham: *nods,* That too.
Sam: I take it you and Lily smoothed things over, then?
Abraham: *grins,* We're getting a divorce.
Sam: I'll raise a glass to that, *orders whiskey for his brother,*

ring-finger's finally getting some air, eh?
Abraham: You know I don't talk that stuff over, but there's news, I'll say that much.
Sam: Stalwart till the bitter end. Some things don't change, do they?
Abraham: Some things, *sighs*, some things never do.

a few awkward moments pass,

Sam: Enosh knows. Now.
Abraham: *raises an eyebrow,* 'Bout you and Jane?
Sam: *nods,* Yea.
Abraham: Does he know about the...other stuff?
Sam: What other stuff?
Abraham: The gambling, those debts, the—
Sam: *hushes him,* Public place, Junior.
Abraham: *nods,* Right, right. *thinks a moment,* Guessing he wasn't over the moon?
Sam: Nope. He was mortified. As he should be.
Abraham: *orders whiskey for his brother,* I'll raise a glass to that.

Whatever son of yours ought to realize what they're in for. Seeing as you never did grow up yourself, can't really see you raising a kid.

Sam: Yea, *stares off,* the truth has a way of coming out as a bad joke sometimes.

Abraham: *sighs,* Ain't that the truth...

Sam: How's Ma doing?

Abraham: *chuckles,* That's a first. Some things really do change. *thinks a moment,* She's getting older, too old to be bitter, I think. She's too soft to yell now, not like she used too, but you know her—she'll keep strong till the Lord comes to take her. *chuckles,* And he better be polite. For his own sake. Why do you ask?

Sam: *shrugs,* Janice thinks we ought to have her come see Enosh some time.

Abraham: *nods,* You should. You know she worries.

Their Drinks Arrive

Sam: *takes his glass,* So what're you gonna do on your own, now that you're a free man?

Abraham: *takes his glass,* I've been stuck in the same place pretty long, too long, it feels. *swirls*

whiskey round glass, think it's 'bout time I wander a bit, be young for a bit.
Sam: *nods,* Amen to that.
Abraham: What about you?
Sam: What about me?
Abraham: You're a father now, what're you gonna do with a son, seeing as you've got one now?
Sam: I've never been one for plans, I've always kept things to today, *shrugs,* never really worried about tomorrow. *swirls whiskey round glass,* Guess I'll stick around, dig some roots, and grow up best I can.
Abraham: *grins,* Amen to that.

Both men raise their glasses, looking into each other's faces. It's the smallest moment, but in it, they see each other in a way they haven't in lifetimes. For the first time in a long time, both can say they have a brother.

Sam: *smiles, raising glass,* To Beginnings.
Abraham: *smiles, raising glass,* To Endings.
Their Glasses Touch
both men drink,
they talk into night,
sharing warm memories,

Cradle Song
by William Blake

Sleep, sleep, beauty bright,
Dreaming in the joys of night;
Sleep, sleep; in thy sleep
Little sorrows sit and weep.

Sweet babe, in thy face
Soft desires I can trace,
Secret joys and secret smiles,
Little pretty infant wiles.

O the cunning wiles that creep
In thy little heart asleep!
When thy little heart doth wake,
Then the dreadful night shall break.

Singing Day Ends

A Divine Image

Cruelty has a Human Heart
And Jealousy a Human Face
Terror the Human Form Divine
And Secrecy, the Human Dress

The Human Dress, is forged Iron
The Human Form, a fiery Forge.
The Human Face, a Furnace seal'd
The Human Heart, its hungry Gorge.

06:06
Four Years Later

It's a typical day's weather, where the unseen windchill undercuts the bright sunbeams that you think ought to make the day so much warmer than it actually is. Often, too often, the weather in the city is a disappointment. Especially in the Fall. God help you in the Winter.

Night approaches with the Sun sinking in the distance. It breaks the horizon's water into hallowed twilight. Enosh walks through this, a backpack over his shoulder, a grin on his face, despite the cold wind smacking his cheeks blushed. Entering the first subway car home, on his last day of highschool and his first day of manhood.

Somewhere in that horizon, the Shepard watches him. As he has, all along, as he promised. Held in place by the shadow of his tombstone, powerless to stop events thousands of miles past his fingertips.

From that hilltop, leaned against an old Oak, he watches, awaiting the inevitable.

Somewhere in that horizon, the mother is with him. Buried beside an old Oak. With the man she'd loved so dearly in life. Her family had saw it only fit that they lay her to rest beside him. She watches on, in her own shadow, powerless to stop events thousands of miles past her fingertips.

From that hilltop, leaned against her husband, she watches, awaiting the inevitable.

Somewhere in that horizon, the daughter is alone. Watching the brother she'd loved with eyes that would—

The twilight's gone. Night's reign begins, the Sun dies, but Enosh rides along in that subway car—oblivious to the darkening of the world outside of it. The inevitable riding his back, an unseen devil in the windchill, an unheard whisper of tragedy in the meaningless crash of rats running down sewers, that invisible hand that holds lost souls in their place tugging on the string of his fate.

In this city of actors, of starless nights, of lost sheep, of salesman, of strays and drunks, of bright lights on pale faces, of lies on honest ears, and gilded promises; *Hush, Hush,* it whispers; This underworld of cursed wealth works on him in silence.

His reflection passes in the glass of the subway car—He's older now, stronger, smarter, and wise as anyone so young can hope to be—Ready to take on the world, and eager to be tested—Oblivious to what awaits him.

He steps out of the subway station nearest home, breathing in the sharp Fall air in late Spring. He spots the lone star hanging from an empty ceiling. Reminded of how Janice had to move away. How she'd told him that her firm was moving, and her job with it, and all the things that owned her—How he'd decided to stay with Sam.

Walking down the street, he passes a few churches and bars. All open and funneling patrons in from the crowded streets—He can't help but think of how Uncle Abraham had stopped going to church. Instead, spending his Sunday nights in rehab centers or Alcoholics Anonymous meetings. Crying on Uncle Sam's doorstep, dumb drunk most nights, cause of the latest woman to break his heart, or leave him broke and hopeless.

Walking up the steps, seeing the cars and a few old women pass by. Bundling up against a cold in their bones. Holding on to their groceries for dear life, on their way home to empty houses—He can't help but think of Ma, and how she'd driven that one rainy night in January, to see him and her sons that had all been sucked into the city. Only to crash.

Looking on the apartment building he'd lived in for the past four years, he couldn't help but think of how she'd left him her home on the lake. Uncle Sam had said they'd be moving out there pretty soon.

The elevator is out of order, so he takes the stairs, and with every step he feels the hairs prickle on his skin. His soul warning, *Halt here, Halt here and spare yourself, Beware him, Beware!, beware, be...ware, be...*

But he does not hear it, not until he turns the doorknob, opens the door of his old home, looks within, and tears his heart open in the same motion.

There are no Angels on these walls—they've been smothered by pale paint over once warm faces—their trumpets choked, their torches drowned, their mouths stuffed with layers of white oblivion.

The Sun is gone, not faded, not blazing, nor there at all, it's been ripped from this room like the heart of a saint—the white paint, over these white walls, is the drying blood of slaughtered Angels.

The strongest smell of weed thickens the air, paired with a bong lying at Uncle Sam's feet. He's passed out over his bed, with an open pill capsule in one hand, and a lit cigarette in the other. He's passed out.

Enosh puts the cigarette out first, checks to see if Sam's alive, which he is, before screwing the cap back on his painkillers. Then he sees it, or rather, he doesn't see it.

>**Enosh:** Where the Hell is my bed?
>**Sam:** *rouses*, Oh. You're home.
>**Enosh:** *looks around*, What did you do?
>**Sam:** *furrows brows*, Didn't I tell you, I'm moving.
>**Enosh:** Yea I know.

Sam: *gestures over the room,* Landlord needed the walls white, *shrugs,* I made 'em white.
Enosh: And my bed?
Sam: *chuckles,* You don't live here anymore.
Enosh: I know, you already said we're moving.
Sam: No. I said *I'm* moving.
Enosh: What's the difference?
Sam: *chuckles,* You.
Enosh: *sighs,* Give me a straight answer or I'm calling the cops. *shakes the pills,* I know these aren't prescription.
Sam: *smirks, hands up in mock surrender,* You got me. Alright, I'll tell you a second time. *drops arms,* Remember when we sat down all civil-like. An' I told you, *deepens voice,* Son, I know you're young. I think it's best if I look after what Ma left you, until you come of age, and when the time comes, I'll move out there. All you gotta do is sign it to me, an' I'll handle the rest?
Enosh: Yea, what about it?
Sam: *sighs, staring into the white ceiling,* Know something—when I was your age, all I wanted was to be my own man. To come out here, and make something of myself. That's why you left too, right? Didn't know what, but you felt like something was out here.

looks to Enosh, Know what I learned as soon as I got out here, on my own?
    Enosh: What'd you learn?
Sam: *giggles,* It's funny, really. Ya see, all the folks back home, everyone's growing up saying "Man, Imma go to the city and *be* somebody", and here, everyone's getting old saying "Man, Imma work real hard to get a house on the lake and *be* somebody." *chuckles,* You see the joke?
    Enosh: *furrows brows,* Kind of, but not really.
    Sam: *whispers,* We're all nobodies. Wherever we go. Nobody cares about you. Nobody cares about me, nobody cares about nobody, and god doesn't care either, *chuckles,* he doesn't care 'bout anybody—Not even Jesus.
    Enosh: Are you okay?
    Sam: *goes on,* Now I knew Ma put that house in your name after Pa died, money in the right pockets gets you that information, so you see, all I wanted was to get back home, swim in that lake, and die there, in peace.
    Enosh: *puts a hand on his Uncle's chest: his heart's racing,* Sam—
Sam: BUT, you see, I've got lots of bad debt, with some worse people. And soon as they knew I had a house in my name, well, *snaps fingers,* it was gone

before I could see it, myself. *chuckles,* Ain't that bitch?! Isn't God funny, Son?!

Enosh: *realizes he's talking to a dying man, eyes widening,* Sam! You need an ambulance!

Sam: *yells, laughing and crying all at once,* Doesn't Jesus love me?! I can feel his love in my fingertips! That sweet release! That numb, numb release!

Enosh: *cries,* Stop! Stop! Please!

Sam: *yells,* Pa can you see me now?! Are you proud?!

Enosh: *sees a festering bite mark on his forearm, almost to himself,* Where's Curiosity?

Sam: *grabs Enosh by his shirt,* I sold the fucking dog...lets go, *shrinking back, seizing up,* I bought those pills with what the bitch was worth.

Enosh: *stares at him long, shock keeping him still a moment, anger making him beat a seizing man the next.*

There's heat, and yelling, and dying; At some point it's too late for either of them.

In the end, Enosh doesn't cry. He sits beside the bed, trying not to see the dead man's hand hanging over the bed's side, or the white walls, or the barred window, or the lake he left, or Janice leaving him, or his Ma driving in the rain, or Uncle Abraham sitting outside of his locked bedroom door, or Big Ma beating Candace, or Ma smacking him to the ground, or himself, or all of it and at some point he stops seeing any of it.

Sitting on a bus-stop bench, watching police cars go by, with all the money he could scavenge in his pockets. He spreads the only book he took with him over his lap. Thinking on better days, humming, *Here Comes the Sun*. He reads that old beaten up Bible that his Pa had given him, staring intensely at the pages.
Keeping his eyes off the thoughts he'd pushed deep under them. He recites verse after verse while the moments crawl into minutes and the sirens blare to shaking intensity, siren's he'd never stop hearing.
He reads, and reads, until morning comes.
knowing that it must all be seen,
he looks to the lone star of an empty sky.
He's looking you in the eye.

A Divine Image

Cruelty has a Human Heart
And Jealousy a Human Face
Terror the Human Form Divine
And Secrecy, the Human Dress

The Human Dress, is forged Iron
The Human Form, a fiery Forge.
The Human Face, a Furnace seal'd
The Human Heart, its hungry Gorge.

by William Blake

End of Novella:
Pretty Women Curse,
Ugly Men Sing

The Enosh Rhapsodies: Book One

Till Next Morning:
Epilogue
XX:XX *His Name was Abraham*

His name is Andrew. He's four years old, with blond hair and blue eyes, just like his mother. Lilith could watch him all day, walking from room to room, looking at things he couldn't understand with all his chubby fingers. His cherub face lighting up at the sight of her, or twisting in pain at every mistake. Like Aphrodite watching Cupid, she loves him beyond love.

The man she'd married shortly after her divorce, for Andrew's sake, was wealthy enough to keep them comfortable and busy enough not to be much of a bother, given that she wasn't very much attracted to the man himself. This, a fact he'd been aware of since their wedding night, but unbothered by.

Lilith sits in a spacious, but empty, living room watching Andrew play out by the water. This is her husband's lakehouse. It has a piano, fur rug, grandfather clock, fireplace, paintings, a few odds and ends, (etc.) but they're all dead inanimate objects with no warmth, not in the fireplace, nor the furniture, not even the bed. With Lilith alone in this room, this house is mostly empty and as materially made up as a well-decorated tomb.

If not for her son she might've considered suicide, or some form of medication to deal with the loss of her first husband. They'd lived together so long that they'd become almost parasitic in marriage. She has no doubt that, at that moment when he'd detached from her, she might've shriveled up and died if Andrew hadn't come into her life, and filled whatever role he abandoned.

She loved being a mother more than she ever enjoyed being a wife, and she was now the warmest in one and coldest in the other. So much so that when her wealthy husband had died, she didn't shed a tear, or attend his funeral—his judgmental mother be damned.

There'd be a day that she'd be sitting here, dead as the couch she sits in, or the book she reads, until Andrew comes running in from outside. With the warmth of his face, her world gets a bit warmer too, and her eyes light up.

Andrew: *walking to her,* Mommy,
Lilith: Yes baby?
Andrew: Where's daddy?
Lilith: *sighs,* That man was not your father.
Andrew: *furrows brows,* What?
Lilith: Your father is far away, that man is dead.
Andrew: He wasn't my daddy?
Lilith: *shakes head,*
Andrew: Why isn't he?
Lilith: *sighs,* Cause mommy doesn't love him like she loves your daddy.
Andrew: *comes closer,* Where is he?

Lilith: *thinks a moment, picking out her words,* He's...fighting in a war.
Andrew: *eyes widen,* He's a general?
Lilith: *smiles, remembering how much he loves his little green army men,* The best there is.
Andrew: Wow, what was he like?
Lilith: *pats her lap, calling him to sit with her,*
Andrew: *scrambles up onto her lap,*
Lilith: *holds him close,* He was like you.
Andrew: Really?
Lilith: *mhms, tickles his arm,* He was strong like you are, *tickles his cheek,* he was sweet like you are, *hugs him tightly,* and I love him sooo much, just like I love you.
Andrew: *giggling,* When's he coming home.
Lilith: *sighs, petting his hair,* I don't know.
Andrew: Why'd he leave?
Lilith: He had his reasons.
Andrew: Can I meet him?
Lilith: *thinks a moment,* One day, but not any time soon.
Andrew: When can I?
Lilith: When you're a man—like he is.

Andrew: *thinks,* Does he not want me?
Lilith: *croons,* No, no, baby, he's just fighting his war, that's all. He'll come home someday.
Andrew: You're sure?
Lilith: Positive.
Andrew: *smiles,* I can't wait.
Lilith: Wanna hear something else about your daddy?
Andrew: *nods, excited,*
Lilith: Okay, I'm gonna tell you a little story.

She tells that story for years. The story of a father who'd never come home. An army man, a lady's man, a scholar and a saint. In part, these were all real stories of a real man she loved, but in truth, they were models for what she wanted of Andrew.

At some point he'd grown unsatisfied with stories, and had begged her for his father's name, over and over again, and at some point she'd given in. With that name came the truth that everything she's told him about his father were partia if not complete lies.

Someday he buys a gun and leaves her to find him. Someday she sinks into that couch for days and weeks and decades, until she's dead to the world.

With no one but herself

His face twisted in a pain she hadn't seen before, at the end of these truths, when she had told him that his father had divorced her while she was pregnant. Whatever pain he would've shown had he known the full truth was too much and she resolved to lie one last time to cover all others.

She says his name was Abraham.

XX:XX *The Last Angel*

The nights are cold, colder than they've ever been, and longer still. The nights are starved, emptier than they've ever been, and quieter still. These nights are sleepless, dreamless, and unending. These nights drown Enosh in their bright lights over dark streets.

He's been wandering for a while now, using up the last of whatever he could gather from the house he ran away from, and the dead man he couldn't call his father. He spends most days in the library, reading there until they close, and politely ask him to leave. Most nights he sits in front of a playgrounds. So that when the morning comes, he can wash his mouth out, and drink from the water fountain.

He carries a few meager possessions with him. The Bible his father had given him, it's pages covered in notes, dashes, and circles, from his countless readings. It was his sinking heart's cane. At some point, he felt like he knew it as well as his Pa had. He could quote verses with a proud nod and a smile—though he hadn't much reason to smile most days.

The obituary section that marks his dead father's funeral date, at a home off a street he'd memorized, is shoved deep into his back pocket. Out of sight, heavier than the Bible he carried in his hands.

Winter is coming, and he's worried for his life. As he has no money left for a coat, or food, or shelter, or even a blanket. Though he's heard of some shelters uptown that might take him. That's where he's heading, now.

That is, until one morning, when out of all the apathetic masses passing him by, one girl stops to talk to him. Rather than give him change, she tells him the secret to redemption.

        Her name is Elisabeth,
the last angel of a starless city.

XX:XX *A Call late into the Night*

Late into the night, miles from the broken cathedral, Janice is awoken by the ring of a phone. When she answers, it's Abraham crying across the line. He's saying words she can't understand—words that don't make sense because they can't register.

Numb to the truth, she takes the first flight home. Chasing yesterday.

Open Letter to all of the Pretty Women I've met:

First and foremost, I thank my Mother. The first pretty woman of my life, and stronger than anyone I can think of. Having me become the man I am is only because you were my mother, and none of this book could've been done without you. I love you.

I'm reminded, at the end of writing this, that a writer is nothing without their English teachers. Hercules was nothing without his tutors as well, and I've been blessed to have so many pretty women to guide me over the past five years of my writing.

To Marta Kargol, who got me into writing in eighth grade, I finally finished a story! Unbelievable right? I wouldn't love books as much as I do, without your in-class library, and I hope you're reading this. Because my writing started with you.

To Lauren Rollens, who taught me that form doesn't come before substance. You've guided my work with an unseen hand for years, and if you look hard enough, I have no doubt you'll see your fingerprints on all my work. I go into the world as a writer, because you've held me to that standard.

To Lina Seaton and Donna Scully, the dynamic duo of my junior year, who taught me to project and speak with something to say, in a way worth listening to. I have to say that you've given my words weight, and I doubt I'll ever forget either of you. I hope this makes up for all the times I showed up without a socratic seminar sheet, but talked more than anyone else, called out, because I couldn't hold my thoughts, or wrote a whole essay, only to ask "There's a prompt?"

To Tracey Gonzalez, who crammed Jane Eyre into my thick skull, and opened up my mind with Cuckoo's nest—I'll be back. Be ready. I might just pop into one of your classes for an unscheduled book signing. I hope I was, at least, an entertaining nuisance. I'm still an asshole with potential, but I'm working on it, for me, and to make you proud.

But more than anyone, anyone on this Earth,
I thank my Papa,
Hipolito Santana,
this one's for you.
It's all for you.
I know you're watching,
from where the heavens kiss the Earth.

this is not goodbye,
this is goodnight.
And I'm gone.

www.ingramcontent.com/pod-product-compliance
Lightning Source LLC
Chambersburg PA
CBHW010447010526
44118CB00021B/2531